Boost your Progress in

Reading and Writing

Sarah Forrest & David White
Series Editor: Alan Howe

HODDER EDUCATION
AN HACHETTE UK COMPANY

Contents

Boost your progress in reading

UNIT 1 Know how to read to understand a text 4
   1 Know how to skim 4   3 Know how to read in detail 12
   2 Know how to scan 8   4 Know how to understand unfamiliar texts 16

UNIT 2 Know how to identify audience and purpose 22
   1 Identify and comment on the audience at which a text is aimed 22   2 Identify and comment on purpose 26

UNIT 3 Know how to understand presentation and organisation 30
   1 Understand presentation and layout 30   2 Know how paragraphs are structured 36

UNIT 4 Know how to write about texts 42
   1 Know how to use quotations 42   3 Know how to write about a text 48
   2 Know how to choose good quotations 44

UNIT 5 Know how to uncover layers of meaning 50
   1 Know how to read between the lines 50   2 Know how to read beyond the lines 58

UNIT 6 Know how to understand points of view 64
   1 Know how to identify fact and opinion 64   3 Know how to identify and comment on points of view 68
   2 Know how to comment on fact and opinion ...66

UNIT 7 Know how to comment on language 72
   1 Know how to comment on the effect of words in a text 72   3 Know how to comment on imagery 80
   2 Know how to comment on sentences in a text 76   4 Know how to comment on rhetorical devices 84

UNIT 8 Know how to share a response to a text 88
   1 Know how to read a text aloud 88   2 Know how to write an essay about a text ... 92

Boost your progress in writing

UNIT 9 Know how to write sentences to interest your reader 96
   1 Know about different types of sentence 96   3 How to write sentences using subordination 102
   2 Know how to use and vary single-clause sentences 100   4 Improve your style by varying your sentences 106

UNIT 10 Know how to use punctuation to make your meaning clear 110
   1 Know how to punctuate sentence boundaries 110   3 Know how to write lists 114
   2 Know how to use commas to make your meaning clear 112   4 Know how to use impact punctuation 118

Contents

UNIT 11 Know how to use paragraphs to organise your writing 120
    1 Know how to use topic sentences 120
    2 Paragraphs and connectives 124

UNIT 12 Know how to use verbs effectively 126
    1 Using verbs so your meaning is clear 126
    2 Using verb tenses 128
    3 Using tricky verbs accurately 130

UNIT 13 Know how to spell words 132
    1 Know how to spell words with quiet or hidden sounds 132
    2 Know how to spell plural nouns 134
    3 Know how to spell verb endings 136
    4 Know how to spell common letter clusters 140
    5 Know how to spell homophones 142
    6 Know how to add suffixes 146

UNIT 14 Know how to choose language to affect your reader 150
    1 Know how to choose words for impact 150
    2 Know how to choose words to match a topic 152
    3 Know how to use writers' techniques 154
    4 Know how to use words and phrases imaginatively 158
    5 Know how to use words with clarity and precision 160
    6 Know how to use words to affect the reader's feelings 162

UNIT 15 Know how to improve and shape your writing 164
    1 Know how to collect ideas and plan 164
    2 Understand the process of writing 166
    3 Know how to edit your writing 168
    4 Know how to add the finishing touches 172

UNIT 16 Know how to focus your writing on audience and purpose 174
    1 Understand the purposes for writing and different kinds of reader 174
    2 Know how to write stories 176
    3 Know how to write instructions 178
    4 Know how to write about something you did 180
    5 Know how to write information texts 182
    6 Know how to write descriptively 184
    7 Know how to write explanations 188
    8 Know how to write to discuss and persuade 190
    9 Know when to use formal and informal writing 194

UNIT 1 Know how to read to understand a text

1 Know how to skim

Learning objective

I am learning how to skim read to understand what a text is about.

Key term

Skim read
Look quickly over the whole text to get an idea of what it is about.

Sometimes you can **skim** a text quickly to get a good idea of what it is about and the key points being made.

Activity 1 Understand how to skim

When you skim read, your eyes move quickly over the words but slow down over the main words that tell you what the text is about. Look at this example, where the main words have been highlighted:

A **venomous tarantula** the **size** of a **human face** has been **found** in a **remote village** in **Sri Lanka**.

1 Skim read this newspaper headline.

> **Careful who you throw snowballs at! Firemen take revenge on teenagers by giving them a drenching with a power hose.**

2 List the main words you remember from skim reading the headline.

Snowballs

...

...

4

Unit 1 Know how to read to understand a text

| Activity 2 | Skim to get the gist of a text |

Key term

Gist
Basic meaning or idea of a text.

1 Skim read this text.

> With the Old Trafford tour you can see the stadium through the eyes of Manchester United greats themselves. From the dizzy heights of the North Stand to Sir Alex Ferguson's pitch-side dugout spot, and the atmosphere-soaked player's dressing room, every experience will seem to carry the roar of the 76,000 fans in your ears.

2 Write down the words that your eyes and mind picked out.

3 Use these words to help you write a short explanation of what the text is about.

From skim reading this text I can see that it is about …

4 Skim read this opening to a magazine article.

> Read Isaac's story:
>
> I was 12 when I first started designing clothing and I did my first collection a year later. I was first inspired to get into fashion when my cousin won a modelling competition. It was the first time I've ever been to a catwalk and the mixture of fashion styles and atmosphere really inspired me.
>
> After that I started doing little drawings and I quite liked it so I decided to get some fabric and started making up dresses. Then from there I just kept doing more and more until about summer 2011 when I decided I wanted to do a catwalk show. I did my first catwalk later in 2011.

5 Notice the main words and write a short explanation of what this text is about.

1 Know how to skim

Activity 3 — Skim to understand the main message of a text

1 Skim read these headings and pictures.

FUNDING THE FUTURE

Should big companies put money towards school sport as well as sport stars?

- a) What main words did you pick out?
- b) What do the pictures show? How do the pictures add to what the text is about?
- c) From skimming the headings and pictures, what do you think the article will be about?

Activity 4 — Skim read to understand the key points in a text

1 The text opposite is from a newspaper article. Skim read the first sentence in paragraph 1. What words do you notice?

2 Skim read the rest of paragraph 1.
- a) What main words do you notice?
- b) What is the key point in paragraph 1?

3 Now, skim read paragraphs 2, 3 and 4. Write a sentence to sum up the key point being made in each paragraph.

4 Read over your summaries of the headings, pictures and paragraphs. Now, sum up the main message of the whole article in one or two sentences.

Unit 1 Know how to read to understand a text

OLYMPIC HERO MO FARAH WILL RUN HALF OF THE LONDON MARATHON IN APRIL – AND GET PAID £250,000 TO DO IT!

The runner, who shot to fame last summer after picking up two gold medals at the London 2012 Games, is being sponsored by Virgin to take part and wear their logo.

Virgin isn't the only huge company to pay a sport star a massive amount of money to advertise its brand. Last month, it was announced that Nike will pay Northern Irish golfer Rory McIlroy £155 million to use its sports kit and equipment for the next ten years. Footballer David Beckham is thought to earn about £13 million through sponsorship with Adidas and other companies each year. Multimillion-pound deals take place every week at the top of sport.

Meanwhile, last week, schools inspector Ofsted said that the standard of sport in schools was too low. 'Pupils were not provided with enough activity to enable them to learn or practise their skills,' complained the UK's chief schools inspector, Sir Michael Wilshaw.

This week, a number of teachers told First News that putting money into school sport is the only way to improve it. They believe funding for PE lessons will play a major part in boosting the number of young people getting into sport after London 2012. 'School sport funding is crucial to the Olympic legacy,' explained Durrington Junior School's Mr Caslin. 'Since the Games last summer, we've had no support!'

Feedback

I can:
→ skim read a text to get the gist of a text
→ skim read to pick out the key points in a text.

2 Know how to scan

Learning objective

I am learning how to scan a text to find information.

> **Key term**
>
> **Scanning**
> Looking quickly over a text to find specific information.

Sometimes you do not need to read every word in a text to find the information you are looking for. Scan by looking through the text to find specific facts or details.

- Use headings and bold print to work out where the information you need is likely to be found in the text.
- Run a finger across each line to search for specific details.
- Then read the whole sentence closely to make sure it is telling you information that you need.

Activity 1 Understand how to scan

Read this short text.

> Born and bred in Scotland, musician Calvin Harris shot to fame with his first album in 2007.

When you scan, look for certain types of words to help you find specific information.

1 Who is this text about?
For **who**, scan for a person's name – capital letters can help you spot this.

> Born and bred in Scotland, musician **Calvin Harris** shot to fame with his first album in 2007.

8

Unit 1 Know how to read to understand a text

2 **Where is Calvin Harris from?**
For **where**, scan for a place name – again, capital letters help with this.

3 **When did he release his first album?**
For **when**, scan for clues to do with time.

| Activity 2 | Scan for specific information |

1 **Scan the text to the right to find out the following information:**

   a) When can you do this activity? Scan for time clues.
   b) Who is the activity suitable for? Scan for types of people mentioned.
   c) Where does the activity take place? Scan for places.

2 a) Scan this passage. Find out who it is about.

> For someone who only started taking a serious interest in acting when he was 15, **Robert Pattinson** – or R-Patz, as some of his friends call him – has had a truly meteoric rise to fame. However, from his screen-stealing performance as **Cedric Diggory** in *Harry Potter and the Goblet of Fire* to his heart-stopping portrayal of **Edward Cullen** in *Twilight*, it's easy to see why. Robert has the rare acting talent and smouldering physical presence all would-be movie stars crave, but few are lucky to possess.

Wednesdays 27 Mar, Thu 6 Jun, Wed 31 Jul, Wed 28 Aug
Children's Explorer Tours
Exciting children's version of our ever popular explorer tours. Brave the darkened tunnels as you go back in time and experience the life of a child during the war.

■ **Air Raid Shelters**
Suitable for ages 7+
6.45pm - 8pm
£3.95 per child,
accompanying adults £2
Booking Essential
Contact: 0161 4741940

   b) There are a lot of names mentioned. Sometimes when you scan, you need to read the information around a word closely to be sure it is the right answer to the question.

This passage is about ...

9

2 Know how to scan

3 What do we find out about Robert?
Scan for information to complete these sentences:

a) Robert is an ...   b) He has been doing this since ...   c) He is most famous for ...

4 How successful is Robert? Scan for words the writer has used to describe him and list them.

- Fame
- Heart-stopping
- ....

Activity 3   Scan for specific details in a text

Look at the leaflet on the next page advertising *The Lion King* stage show.

1 Scan the text in the leaflet to find out when and where you can see the show.

2 a) Scan the text to find out what you would see if you went to see the show.

List the information.
- Music – African songs, rhythms
- ...
- ...

b) Scan for words in the leaflet that tell you the show will be good. List them.
- thrilling
- sell-out
- ...

3 What do other people think of the show? Scan for reviews of the show by looking for quotations – you can scan quickly for these by looking for quotation marks.

Sum up in your own words what other people think of the show.

Unit 1 Know how to read to und...

**SELL-OUT SEASON MUST END 20 APRIL
LIMITED SEATS MAY STILL BE AVAILABLE**

PALACE THEATRE

'PREPARE TO BE AMAZED!
A SIMPLY GLORIOUS EXPERIENCE'
Oldham Evening Chronicle

'A GENUINE BLOCKBUSTER RIGHT ON OUR DOORSTEP!
Pulsating rhythms and hauntingly beautiful African songs'
Manchester Evening News

Disney presents

THE LION KING
THE AWARD-WINNING MUSICAL

Disney's *The Lion King* has been thrilling audiences and critics alike at Manchester's Palace Theatre, as it plays to sell-out crowds and standing ovations.

Based on the beloved film, Julie Taymor's legendary production uses pure theatrical magic to tell the story of Simba - transporting audiences of all ages with its dazzling stagecraft, innovative use of masks and puppets and the evocative rhythms of Africa.

This strictly limited season must end 20 April so book your tickets now to catch 'THE MUST-SEE SHOW OF THE YEAR' TOWER FM.

UNTIL SAT 20 APR
Tue-Sat eves 7.30pm
Wed, Sat & Sun mats 2.30pm
Extra mats Thu 4 & Thu 18 Apr

TICKETS £20-£55
(Premium seats £72.50 & £75)

ATG TICKETS
0844 871 3019 (bkg fee)
www.atgtickets.com/manchester

3

4 What do you find out about *The Lion King* show from this leaflet? Piece together all the details you have scanned and sum up the leaflet in one to two sentences.

From this leaflet I can see that 'The Lion King' is ...

Feedback

I can:
➔ scan for specific information
➔ scan to understand a whole text.

11

Know how to read in detail

Learning objective — *I am learning to read a text carefully and closely.*

Sometimes you will have to read a text slowly and closely to understand it. You can use two techniques to help you do this: the 5 Ws and visualisation.

Activity 1 — Use the 5 Ws: who, where, what, when and why

Look at this headline, picture and caption.

LAD, 2, RESCUED AFTER TODDLING ONTO ROOF 40FT ABOVE GROUND

Drama … Preston Likely grabs onto a two-year-old child atop the country hotel

Unit 1 Know how to read to understand a text

1 Find out the details of the story.

   a) Who is the story about?

   > The story is about a two-year-old boy and ...

   b) Where did the story take place?

   c) What is the story about?

   d) Why did the story take place?

Activity 2 — Find more details

Now read the full newspaper article.

THIS IS THE DRAMATIC MOMENT A HEROIC PASSER-BY RESCUED A TWO-YEAR-OLD BOY STUCK 40FT ABOVE THE GROUND – AFTER HE TODDLED ONTO A HOTEL ROOF.

Preston Likely, 42, scrambled up a drainpipe to reach the stricken tot after spotting him perched on the top of the pitched roof.

The little boy's panicked mother had tried to rescue him but became stuck herself as she tried to reach her son.

Incredibly, the boy, named only as Charlie, had scaled a 20ft-high ladder before climbing up the steep roof of the Tree Hotel near Oxford.

Guests were enjoying an evening drink in the beer garden late last Saturday afternoon when they spotted Charlie above them.

Dad-of-one Preston dashed to the boy's rescue, scrambling up the front of the building and held onto the struggling boy for 15 minutes before fire crews arrived.

Preston, an artist and author who lives in Oxford, said: 'I was about to sit down when I noticed a large crowd of people staring at something.

'I thought it was some sort of gathering. Then I looked up and saw the child on the roof tottering about.

'I threw my bag down without thinking and just climbed up and grabbed him. It was instinctive, I didn't think, I just scrambled up.

'He was wriggling about, and for a two-year-old was very powerful.

'It made it all the more precarious and I really had to squeeze to hold onto the little guy.'

1 Search each paragraph for all the details about **who, where, when, what** and **why**.

3 Know how to read in detail

2 As you read, record all the details about **who** in a table.

| Who | Little boy: 2 years old, called Charlie, was with his mother, climbed onto the roof
Rescuer: |
|---|---|
| Where | |
| When | |
| What | |
| Why | |

Key term

Visualise
To use the words in a text to create a picture in your mind of what is happening.

Activity 3　Visualise the details

1 Read this passage from *Frankenstein*. It describes the moment when the scientist realises that he has created another being.

What do you know about … *Frankenstein*?

Frankenstein is a gothic horror story by Mary Shelley which was written in 1818. It tells the story of a scientist – Victor Frankenstein – who creates and brings to life a monster.

It was on a dreary night of November that I beheld the **accomplishment** of my **toils**. With an **anxiety** that almost amounted to agony, I collected the instruments of life around me, that I might infuse a spark of being into the lifeless thing that lay at my feet. It was already one in the morning; the rain pattered dismally against the panes, and my candle was nearly burnt out, when, by the glimmer of the half-extinguished light, I saw the dull yellow eye of the creature open; it breathed hard, and a **convulsive** motion agitated its limbs.

Expand your vocabulary

accomplishment – result
toils – hard work
anxiety – worry, nervousness
convulsive – jerking, shaking

Unit 1 Know how to read to understand a text

a) Visualise where and when the story is set. Sum up what you can see.

> I can picture a dark room. It is cold and ...

b) List five different words and phrases that helped you visualise this place in detail.
- Dreary night
- November
- ...
- ...
- ...

2 **Read the passage again. Find details about who is in the story.**

> It was on a dreary night of November that I beheld the accomplishment of my toils.

Key term

Narrator
The person who is telling the story in the first person, using 'I'.

There is a narrator and who else?

3 a) Find the words and phrases that tell you the narrator is doing an experiment.

b) Explain what the experiment is.

4 a) Find the words that tell you how the narrator is feeling.

b) Sum up in your own words how the narrator is feeling.

Feedback

I can:
→ use the 5 Ws to find and explain details in a text
→ use visualisation and my understanding of words to picture the details.

15

4 Know how to understand unfamiliar texts

Learning objective

I am learning to:
- understand why a text might be difficult to understand
- use my knowledge and experience to understand a text.

Focus your effort

Link unfamiliar words to other words that you already know. Using your prior understanding and experience is an important skill and will help you get to grips with tricky texts.

Sometimes a text may be difficult to read because it has unfamiliar words and long, complicated sentences. Take your time and read each word carefully, thinking about what you already know, and use the other words and sentences in the text to understand it.

Activity 1 — Understand why a text seems difficult

1 Read this text. Which of the features listed in the box on the left makes it difficult to understand? What features help you understand it?

- long sentences
- pictures
- bullet points
- difficult words
- lots of writing
- use of colour

Plate movement

The Earth's core is extremely hot. Heat escapes from the core and rises up into the mantle. This heat causes **Convection currents** in the semi-solid rocks of the mantle. The convection currents cause the mantle rock to move very slowly in a circular motion. The movement of the rock in the mantle drags the tectonic plates along (Fig 2). In this way, the tectonic plates move by a few centimetres every year. In our lifetimes the plates will only move a few metres. But over million of years, plates can move the whole way around the Earth! This process is called **plate tectonics**. It explains how the continents, which used to be joined together, have spread apart.

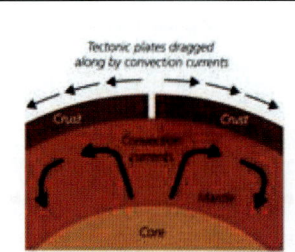

Fig 2 Movement of tectonic plates

▶ **Q3** What causes convection currents?

Earthquakes and volcanoes

Fig 1 shows the location of the world's major volcanoes and earthquake zones. It shows that earthquakes and volcanoes are found together in long narrow bands. For example, there is a large land of volcanoes and earthquake sites around the Pacific Ocean. This band is known as the 'Ring of Fire'. Notice how close the bands of earthquakes and volcanoes are to where the tectonic plates meet. This map shows us that most earthquakes and volcanoes occur at **plate boundaries** (Fig 3). Earthquakes and volcanoes can be very useful for learning about the movements of the Earth's crust.

▶ *Fig 3* San Andreas fault - an example of a plate boundary

Unit 1 Know how to read to understand a text

| Activity 2 | Use your prior knowledge of texts |

1 This page is taken from a secondary school geography textbook.

   a) Record what you already know about textbooks.

   b) Find examples of these features in this text. Add these to the table.

   c) How do these features help you to understand the text? Complete the table.

Features of textbooks	Example from this text	How this can help me understand the text
Headings	Tectonic processes at the top of page Plate movement	Sums up what the page will be about Tells us what that section is about
Pictures	Labelled diagram …	
Bold writing		

• •

| Activity 3 | Tackle unfamiliar words |

1 a) The word 'plate' is important in understanding the meaning of this text. How do you know it is an important word?

   b) The word 'plate' has a different meaning here than the one you are most familiar with. How can your understanding of the word 'plate' help you understand this text?

2 Find these three words in the text that you probably already know the meaning of.

   • boundaries – *helps me understand that the text is about different areas*
   • band
   • crust

   How can the ordinary meaning of each word help you understand the academic meaning of each word in this text?

17

4 Know how to understand unfamiliar texts

3 a) Use a dictionary or glossary to find out the meaning of any words in the text about which you are still unsure.

b) Record the definitions.

4 Use the notes you have made to sum up in 50 words what this text is about.

Activity 4 | **Understand texts from other cultures**

When reading a text from a different time, place or culture, use what you already know and understand to help you figure out the meaning of unfamiliar words. You should also think about when, where and why the text was written to help you understand its meaning. You can also use dictionaries and the internet to look up tricky words and ideas.

1 Read the opening to the poem.

Expand your vocabulary

embossed – printed, patterned

Presents from my Aunts in Pakistan

They sent me a salwar kameez
    peacock-blue,
        and another
    glistening like an orange split open,
embossed slippers, gold and black
    points curling.
Candy-striped glass bangles
    snapped, drew blood.
Like at school, fashions changed
    in Pakistan –
the salwar bottoms were broad and stiff,
    then narrow.
My aunts chose an apple-green sari,
    silver-bordered
        for my teens.

Unit 1 Know how to read to understand a text

2 Read the poem again, and answer the following questions.

   a) What kind of presents are sent from Pakistan?

   b) What words from the text help you understand this?

3 The following words are specific to a particular place and culture.

salwar kameez   sari

   a) Do you know what these words mean?

   b) Use a dictionary or internet search engine to find out their meaning.

4 How does the writer help people understand what the salwar kameez and sari are like?

Activity 5 Understand texts from other times

1 Read this text from the play *Romeo and Juliet*.

> *Enter TYBALT*
>
> **TYBALT**   What, art thou drawn among these heartless hinds? Turn thee, Benvolio, look upon thy death.
>
> **BENVOLIO** I do but keep the peace: put up thy sword, Or manage it to part these men with me.
>
> **TYBALT**   What, drawn, and talk of peace! I hate the word, As I hate hell, all Montagues, and thee: Have at thee, coward!
>
> *They fight*

What do you know about … *Romeo and Juliet*?

Romeo and Juliet is a play written by William Shakespeare around 1595. It tells the story of two young people who fall in love, even though their families hate each other.

4 Know how to understand unfamiliar texts

2 **Use your knowledge and experience to help you understand.**

   a) What do you notice about the layout of the text?

   b) Which words are familiar?

   c) Use this understanding to write a sentence explaining what you think is happening in the extract.

3 **The word 'art' here is an archaic word for 'are'.**

   a) Find another archaic word or phrase.

   b) Match these archaic words to the modern version.

thee	put down
look upon	your
put up	you
thy	get ready to see

   c) Re-write this line so it makes more sense to a modern reader.

   > Turn thee, Benvolio, look upon thy death.

4 **a)** The word 'drawn' has different meanings. Which of these meanings is correct for this extract?

   | looking tired | closed curtains | pulling a weapon out |

   b) What other words in the text help you understand this?

5 **When Tybalt says 'heartless hinds' he is talking about a group of servants that have been arguing.**

   a) What two words do you find if you break the word 'heartless' up? Use what you already understand about these words to write down what heartless means.

   b) Where have you heard the word 'hind' before? What do you think it means?

   c) Use a dictionary to look up any of these words if you are still unsure.

   d) Use your understanding of these words to explain what Tybalt is saying when he calls the servants 'heartless hinds'.

Key term

Archaic
Very old, old-fashioned, no longer used.

Unit 1 Know how to read to understand a text

6 How might you find out the meaning of any other words in the extract you are still unsure of?

7 Use the notes you have made to re-write the extract in modern language.

Feedback

I can:

→ identify why texts are difficult to read

→ use my prior knowledge and experience to understand tricky texts.

21

UNIT 2
Know how to identify audience and purpose

1 Identify and comment on the audience at which a text is aimed

Learning objective

I am learning to:
- identify the audience at which a text is aimed
- comment on how a text attracts an audience.

Focus your effort

Skim read a text to identify the audience. Then think carefully about how the text attracts that audience through the choices the writer has made over language and presentation.

Most texts are written with an audience in mind. Writers make choices about topic, presentation and language so that their texts attract and are matched to the right audience.

Activity 1 — Use topic to identify audience

Think about these four texts:

- a leaflet for a garden centre
- an advert for denture cream
- a recipe for a family shepherds' pie
- packaging for Coco Pops cereal.

Key terms

Audience
The specific group or groups of people a text has been written for.

Topic
What a text is about.

1 Use the topic of each text to decide which of these audiences each is aimed at:

a) Parents
b) Elderly people
c) Children
d) Gardeners

22

Unit 2 Know how to identify audience and purpose

| Activity 2 | Use presentation to identify audience |

Look carefully at this image.

1 What do you notice about what this image looks like?

Presentation feature	Example from text
Colours	Pink, purple, pastel colours
Pictures	
Words	
Logo	

2 What age group will this image attract? Use ideas from your table to explain why.

primary school children   teenagers   grandparents

3 What gender will this image attract? Explain why.

male   female

23

1 Identify and comment on the audience at which a text is aimed

Activity 3 — Use the language of a text to identify audience

Read this extract from *Diary of a Wimpy Kid*.

What do you know about … *Diary of a Wimpy Kid*

Diary of a Wimpy Kid is a comedy novel by Jeff Kinney about a boy called Greg and his troubles and adventures at middle school. It is written in the style of a diary and uses words and cartoon images to tell the story.

Key terms

Colloquial language
Informal words and phrases: the chatty, relaxed way you speak with your friends and family, or how you write when you text or email them.

Writing in the first person
Writing using 'I' or 'we' as the subject, for example: I went to the concert.

> The only reason I agreed to do this at all is because I figure later on when I'm rich and famous, I'll have better things to do than answer people's stupid questions all day long. So this book is gonna come in handy.
>
> GREGORY! TELL US ABOUT YOUR CHILDHOOD!
> WERE YOU ALWAYS SO SMART AND HANDSOME?
> HERE'S MY JOURNAL. NOW SHOO, SHOO.
> FLASH
>
> Like I said, I'll be famous one day, but for now I'm stuck in high school with a bunch of morons.
>
> MORONS

1 Find three examples of colloquial language.

2 What age group would this colloquial language attract?

| adults | teenagers | toddlers |

Explain why.

3 a) Find an example of use of the first person.

b) Find an example of humour.

c) Why do these language features also attract this target audience?

4 How does the topic and presentation of this text also attract this audience?

Unit 2 Know how to identify audience and purpose

Activity 4 — Comment on how a text attracts a specific audience

Look at these two news websites:

www.bbc.co.uk/newsround/

www.bbc.com/news/

1 What audience do you think each one is aimed at?

> Text 1 is aimed at … Text 2 is aimed at …

2 Record the features that have been used in each text.

Features	Text 1	Text 2
Topics	Music, football, quizzes	
Presentation and layout		Pictures and writing in equal amounts, pictures quite small, not a lot of colour – mainly red, black, white, grey
Language – words used		

3 Write a paragraph about the BBC Newsround website, explaining how the features attract the audience.

Write a sentence or two:
- explaining who the website is aimed at
- explaining how the topics attract this audience
- explaining how the presentation attracts this audience
- explaining how the language attracts this audience.

4 Write a paragraph about Text 2, explaining how the features attract its audience.

> Text 2 is aimed at … The topics covered on this web page are … This would appeal to … because … The text also uses …

Feedback

I can:
→ identify the target audience of a text
→ understand what choices a writer has made to attract an audience.

25

2 Identify and comment on purpose

Learning objective

I am learning to:
→ *identify the purpose of a text*
→ *comment on how a text achieves its purpose.*

Key term

Purpose
Why a text has been written. A novel, for example, is written to entertain.

Most texts are written to achieve a purpose. Writers make choices about the presentation, layout and language they will use to achieve their purpose.

Activity 1 — Understand different purposes

Focus your effort

Skim read a text to identify the purpose quickly. Think carefully about the choices the writer has made about language and features of presentation to achieve that purpose.

1 Match each text to its purpose.

1	a recipe	a)	entertain
2	a play	b)	explain
3	a diary	c)	persuade
4	a textbook	d)	instruct
5	an advert	e)	recount

Activity 2 — Use language and layout to identify purpose

GO FOR IT: TELL EVERYONE

Posting information about your podcast on an internet forum or message board is easy and free:
- Search the internet for forums and message boards that concentrate on the subject of your podcast.
- Sign-up for an account.
- Post a new message telling other forum users about your podcast.

Read this text. It is taken from a 'how to' guide.

1 Find the bullet points. Why have they been used?

2 a) Which of these types of sentence has been used in the heading?

   a question   a command   a statement

   b) What type of sentence has been used in each of the bullet points?

   c) Why have these sentences been used?

Unit 2 Know how to identify audience and purpose

3 Use the information about the text that you have just gathered to decide whether the purpose of this text is to:

a) entertain
b) explain
c) persuade
d) instruct
e) recount.

4 a) Which of these features of language and presentation have been used?

short sentences	added detail	encouraging words
complex words	images	bright colours

b) Explain how they help achieve the purpose. For example:

> Short sentences help to achieve the purpose because they make the instructions easy to read and follow.

Activity 3 — Understand how writers achieve purpose

1 Read the opening of the novel *Fat Boy Swim*, by Catherine Forde. What is its main purpose?

'Oi, boobsy. Move your fat butt! We're under pressure here.'

One rasp from Maddo McCormack in goals was enough to set Jimmy stumbling up the pitch, as though someone had given him a wedgie up the backside.

He only shuffled half a dozen steps, each one making his thick flesh judder. The impact of his foot hitting the ground had him wheezing like an old accordion.

It was hopeless. Pointless. Jimmy halted. Leaned forward, hands on knees.

Gasping.

Knackered.

What do you know about … *Fat Boy Swim*?

Fat Boy Swim is a novel by Catherine Forde about an overweight teenager called Jimmy. Jimmy loves to cook and is challenged by a school coach to take up swimming to get fit.

27

2 Identify and comment on purpose

2 How does the author use language to achieve the purpose? Use examples from the text.

3 Write a sentence or two about each language feature, explaining how it achieves the purpose. For example:

> The author opens with some direct speech and I think this is entertaining because it makes us feel like we're really there as part of the action. The words in the speech are also quite funny and it makes us laugh …

Activity 4 — Comment on how texts achieve different purposes

Skim read these two texts.

Text 1

Magic Kingdom Park at a glance	
Location	Off World Drive, Walt Disney World
Size	107 acres/43ha in 7 'lands'
Hours	9am–7pm off peak; 9am–10pm President's Day (see page 19), spring school holidays; 9am–midnight high season (Easter, summer holidays, Thanksgiving and Christmas)
Admission	Under-3s free; 3-9 $60 (1-Day base ticket), $272 (5-Day Premium), $276 (7-Day Premium); adult (10+) $71, $310, $314, Prices do not include tax.
Parking	$10
Lockers	Next to stroller and wheelchair hire $7 ($2 deposit refunded)
Pushchairs	$10 and $18 (Stroller Shop to right of main entrance); length of stay price varies
Wheelchairs	$10 or $40 ($5 deposit refunded) (Main Ticket Centre)
Top Attractions	Splash Mountain, Space Mountain, Mickey's PhilharMagic, Big Thunder Mountain Railroad, Pirates of the Caribbean, most rides in Fantasyland
Don't Miss	Disney Dreams Come True Parade, SpectroMagic Parade (certain nights) and Wishes fireworks (most nights)
Hidden Costs	**Meals** Burger, Chips and coke $8.98; 3-course dinner $40 (Cinderella's Table); Kids' meal $3.99–7.49
	T-shirts $20–32
	Souvenirs $1–37,500
	Sundries Face painting $8–15, or silhouettes $8, with oval frame $15.95

Text 2

Magic Kingdom Park

Wonder and fantasy are everywhere. Six enchanted lands with over 40 magical attractions make exciting adventures and timeless fairy tale classics just a smile away. It's the one–and only–place where once upon a time is now, and make-believe is as real as today.

Fun for little ones
- **New Fantasyland**: the largest expansion in the history of Magic Kingdom Park
- **Buzz Lightyear's Space Ranger Spin** (inspired by Disney-Pixar's 'Toy Story'): save the toy universe and travel to infinity and beyond.
- **"It's a small world"** sail off on a Disney classic

Big thrills
- **Big Thunder Mountain Railroad**: take off on a runaway train through the Wild West!
- **Space Mountain**: roller coaster adventure into the darkest part of the universe
- **Splash Mountain**: soak up a five storey drop on this hugely popular ride

Family fun
- **Monsters Inc. Laugh Floor** (inspired by Disney-Pixar's 'Monsters Inc.'): get the giggles going strong enough to power Monstropolis
- **The Magic, The Memories and You!**: a nightly projection show that transforms Cinderella Castle into a shimmering canvas of images of guests from that day
- **Wishes**™: the night-time spectacular 'story in the sky'
- **Mickey's PhilharMagic:** Disney music meets Disney magic at this outrageous 3D extravaganza

TOP TIPS!
- If you have little ones, head straight for Fantasyland for attractions the whole family can enjoy together.
- Check out the Tip Board on Main Street, U.S.A. throughout the day–it'll give you an idea of the attraction wait times and help plan your day.
- For a superb view of **Wishes**™, the night-time musical of fireworks spectacular, stand on Main Street, U.S.A facing Cinderella Castle. Alternatively, watch the whole show while dining at the California Grill at the very top of Disney's Contemporay Resort.

Unit 2 **Know how to identify audience and purpose**

1 Quickly identify the purpose of each one.

> The purpose of Text 1 is to … Whereas Text 2 is written to …

2 Re-read each text carefully, in detail. Look at the language and layout in each text. How are they similar and different?

Features	Differences		Similarities
	Text 1	Text 2	
Presentation and layout			Both separate the information using a table or bullet points
Language – words used	Lots of numbers – times and prices		
Sentences – length, type		Some commands	

3 Text 2 is written to persuade. Do you think it might also have another purpose?

4 Write a paragraph about Text 1 explaining:
- what the purpose(s) is
- how presentation and layout achieve the purpose
- how language achieves the purpose
- how the sentences achieve the purpose.

5 Write a paragraph about Text 2 explaining how the features you have identified achieve the purpose(s).

> Text 2 is written to … This is partly achieved through presentation. The writer uses …

Feedback

I can:
→ identify the main purpose of a text
→ understand what choices a writer has made to achieve its purpose.

29

UNIT 3 Know how to understand presentation and organisation

1 Understand presentation and layout

Learning objective

I am learning to:

→ identify how texts are presented and laid out to help the reader

→ comment on how presentation and layout are used.

Many texts use presentation and layout to attract an audience and achieve a purpose. In this section you will learn about different ways that writers do this.

Activity 1 Notice presentation and layout

1 Look at the advert on the opposite page and find each of these features:

- Colour
- Pictures
- Logo
- Bold writing
- Capital letters

2 What do you notice about the presentation? Write a sentence about each of these features. Select words from the box to help you.

a) Colour

There are a variety of different colours used but they are all very bright and eye-catching.

b) Pictures

c) Writing

d) Logo

Key terms

Presentation
How a text looks. This includes visual features such as colour, images and font.

Layout
How a text is arranged, where different parts of the text (for example pictures, writing) are placed on the page.

Logo
An image or symbol that is linked to a product or company.

Product
A thing that is being sold.

Focus your effort

Look carefully at how a text is presented and laid out. Comment on why these choices have been made by linking each feature to the audience and purpose of the text.

Unit 3 Know how to understand presentation and organisation

cartoon	bold	bright	variety
colourful	capitals	funny	

3 What do you notice about the layout? Which statements are right?

The logo is positioned at the top of the advert.

There is more writing than images.

The images are positioned in the centre of the advert.

The images are bigger than the writing.

The details about the place are at the top of the advert.

The advert uses borders and banners around the writing.

The logo is very small in the bottom right-hand corner.

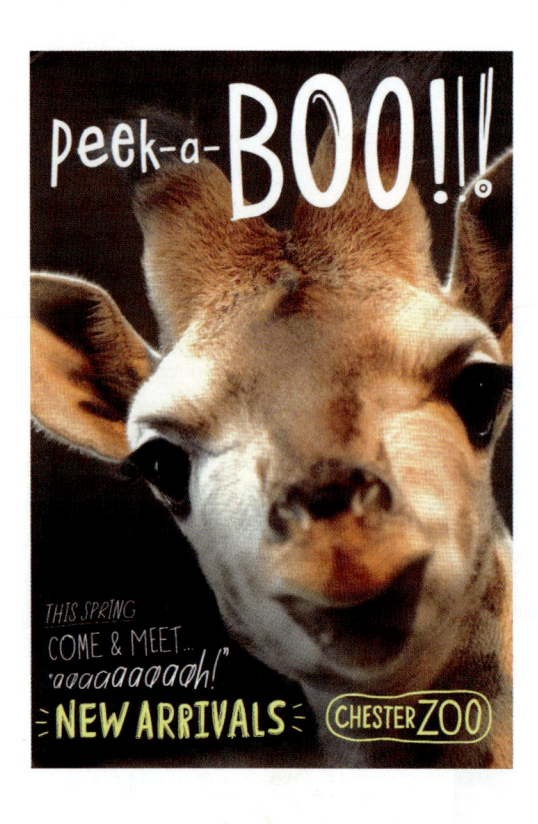

1 Understand presentation and layout

Activity 2 — **Comment on presentation and layout**

1 Look at the leaflet on the left. What do you notice about its presentation and layout?

Presentation	Layout
Large picture, close-up photo of giraffe's face	In centre, takes up most of the space
Natural colours	
Product logo	

2 Why has the writer made these choices? Match each feature with the most likely reason for that choice.

1 There is a large, close-up photograph of a giraffe's face in the centre of the text.

2 The colours used are very natural.

3 The product logo is in yellow and is positioned in the bottom right-hand corner.

4 Bold, capital letters are used for most of the writing.

a) This stands out from the other writing and will be the last thing the reader sees so it will stick in their mind.

b) This means that nothing detracts from the main images and also makes the zoo seem a very calm, natural place to visit.

c) This makes you notice and read the main points on the text.

d) People are often attracted to images of animals so this makes them take notice.

3 Write out this passage, filling the gaps with words from the box.

powerful   large
cute   photograph
encourage   stands
remember   bold
logo   emotions

The _____ image of a _____ giraffe is _____ as it grabs the reader's attention and appeals to their _____. The _____ is of a real animal and will _____ people to go to the zoo to see it. The writing is mostly in _____ or capitals so it _____ out. The product _____ is the last thing readers will see at the bottom of the leaflet so that they will _____ the name of the place.

32

Unit 3 Know how to understand presentation and organisation

Activity 3 — Understand why presentation and layout choices have been made

Key terms

Target audience
The group of people that a text is written for.

Purpose
The reason a text has been written, for example: to persuade, to entertain.

1 Look at this leaflet. Find these features:

- Heading
- Sub-headings
- Bullet points
- Background

You don't have to wait until you're 17 to get behind the wheel of a car!

If you are 11-17 years old you can learn to drive at one of our specialist centres.

Let our fully qualified, government approved driving instructors show you how to:

start / drive / reverse / brake / corner / park and steer in a dual control Skoda Citigo.

Why do we encourage 11-17 year olds to drive?
One in five newly qualified drivers will crash within 6 months of passing their test
Newly qualified drivers and their passengers account for one in five UK road deaths
In Sweden, accident rates were slashed by 40% when drivers had lessons at an earlier age

How much?
Lessons cost just £31.99 for 30 minutes and £59.95 for 1 hour. Gift voucher packs available. Birthday parties/groups from £99.99 for 6 people.

Learn to drive at a venue near you:
London, Birmingham, Bluewater, Bristol, Newcastle, Glasgow, Southampton and Sheffield.

Join us on facebook:
www.facebook.com/youngdrivers

"Can't wait to drive again"
"I reverse parked on my first lesson"

To book go to
www.youngdriver.eu
or call **0844 371 9010**

33

1 Understand presentation and layout

2 a) Find three more presentation features.

   b) Find three more layout features.

3 Which features attract the audience of 11–17-year-olds?

4 Which features help the leaflet to persuade?

5 a) Why has the writer used photographs instead of drawings?

   b) What details do you notice about the photos? Why has the writer made these choices?

6 Complete the table. Explain the effect of the leaflet's presentation and layout.

Feature	Effect
Lots of photographs of young people driving and smiling	Makes it seem like they are having a great time – other people will want to do the same so they will go for a driving lesson here.
Pictures are big, they take up most of the space	
Lots of bright colours	

Activity 4 — Comment on effect

1 Read this student's response about the effect of this leaflet.

> The text is a leaflet that persuades teenagers to have a driving lesson with this company. It also gives the reader a bit of information about how much it will cost and where you can do it.
>
> The leaflet uses the colour red, which is good because it attracts the readers' attention. There are also lots of images of young people so that teenagers know the leaflet is for them.
>
> The leaflet has a heading that attracts the readers' attention. The images are good because teenagers like looking at pictures.

Unit 3 Know how to understand presentation and organisation

2 Find the comments the student has made about:

a) presentation c) purpose

b) layout d) audience.

3 Read the teacher's comments about this student's response.

> Well done! You make some clear points. However, I would like you to re-write your response, making sure you:
> - avoid repeating 'good' and 'attracts the readers' attention'
> - make one more comment about layout
> - make two more comments about presentation.

4 Re-write and improve the student's response, taking note of the teacher's comments.

Feedback

I can:
→ identify features of presentation and layout in a text
→ comment on their effect.

35

2 Know how paragraphs are structured

Learning objective

I am learning to:
- understand how writing can be organised into paragraphs
- understand how paragraphs are linked together.

Focus your effort

Notice what types of words and sentences writers use to link and sequence their ideas, then comment on the effect of the techniques used.

Writers of prose texts organise their words carefully into sentences and paragraphs. In this section you will find out how ideas are organised into paragraphs and how paragraphs are linked in whole texts.

Key terms

Clause
A group of words containing key elements such as a verb.

Sentence
A group of words that may consist of a single clause or may contain several clauses held together by subordination or coordination.

Topic sentence
The first sentence in a paragraph; it introduces what the paragraph will be about.

Sentence using subordination
A sentence with a main clause and at least one subordinate clause.

Single-clause sentence
A sentence with a single main clause.

Time connective
A word or phrase that tells us when something happens.

Direct speech
The words that are spoken by a character in a story.

Activity 1: Understand how paragraphs use effective opening sentences

Read this extract from the novel *We Bought a Zoo*. It is from a chapter about the family's adventures when they first moved to the zoo.

> But then, four days after we took over Dartmoor Wildlife Park, while chatting to Rob about what to do with our **surplus** stock, the unthinkable happened. One of the most dangerous animals on the park, Sovereign, was accidentally let out of his **enclosure** by a **catastrophic** blunder from a junior keeper. At about 5.30 pm I was sitting with Rob in the kitchen when Duncan burst in, shouting, 'ONE OF THE BIG CATS IS OUT. THIS IS NOT A DRILL,' and then ran off again. Now, Duncan doesn't normally shout, or get agitated, but here he was clearly doing both. Rod disappeared like a puff of smoke, and I knew he had gone to get the guns and organise the staff's response. I sat for an increasingly surreal moment, and then decided that, as director of the zoo I probably ought to go and see exactly what was going on. I started making my way towards the part of the park where the big lions are kept.

Unit 3 Know how to understand presentation and organisation

This was one of the strangest moments of my life. All I knew was that a big cat – a lion, a tiger? – was out, somewhere and may be about to come bounding round the corner like an energetic Tigger, but not nearly so much fun. I saw a shovel and picked it up, but it felt like an anvil in my hand. What was the point? I thought, and dropped it, and began walking towards the sound of screaming. Was I about to see someone being eaten alive? I had images of someone still alive but fatally mauled, ribcage asunder, being consumed before a horrified audience. Then a car pulled up with Duncan and Robert in it. 'GET IN THE CAR!' I was told, and gladly complied.

What do you know about ... autobiography?

An autobiograpy is an account of someone's life, written by that person. *We Bought a Zoo* is an autobiography by Benjamin Lee and gives an account of the time he and his family went to live and work at a run-down zoo.

1 Think about the topic sentence.

Extract 1

But then, four days after we took over Dartmoor Wildlife Park, while chatting to Rob about what to do with our surplus stock, the unthinkable happened.

Expand your vocabulary

surplus – left-over
enclosure – cage
catastrophic – terrible

Complete the table to show what you find out from this sentence.

Who	Rob
What	
Where	Dartmoor Wildlife Park
When	

2 a) How would you describe this topic sentence?

long   short   single-clause   multi-clause

b) Why has the writer written the sentence this way?

3 Which words in the topic sentence make you want to read on? Explain why.

2 Know how paragraphs are structured

Activity 2 — **Understand how paragraphs continue**

Read the sentences that follow the topic sentence.

> **Extract 2**
>
> One of the most dangerous animals on the park, Sovereign, was accidentally let out of his enclosure by a catastrophic blunder from a junior keeper. At about 5.30 pm I was sitting with Rob in the kitchen when Duncan burst in, shouting, 'ONE OF THE BIG CATS IS OUT. THIS IS NOT A DRILL,' and then ran off again.

1 How does this information link to the topic sentence? Select which of these answers explains this best:

- It tells us what the 'unthinkable' is.
- It gives us more information about who is involved.
- It describes the wildlife park.

2 a) The topic sentence uses the time connective 'four days after' to give information about **when**. Find another time connective in this extract which gives additional information about when something happened.

b) Why has the writer used these time connectives?

3 a) Besides **when**, what else do you find out from this extract? Complete the table.

Who	
What	
Where	
Why	

4 Which words or phrases make you want to read on? Explain why.

> The phrase 'most dangerous animals' makes me want to read on because it sounds like something really bad could happen – I want to read on to find out if everyone's okay.

5 Find the direct speech. Why does the writer include this?

> The direct speech is … I think the writer uses this because …

Unit 3 Know how to understand presentation and organisation

> **Activity 3** Understand how paragraphs end

Read this extract from the end of the paragraph.

Extract 3

Was I about to see someone being eaten alive? I had images of someone still alive but fatally mauled, ribcage asunder, being consumed before a horrified audience. Then a car pulled up with Duncan and Robert in it. 'GET IN THE CAR!' I was told, and gladly complied.

1 a) When a paragraph ends it signals that there is going to be a change. Do the words 'GET IN THE CAR!' tell you there will be a change of:

| time? | topic? | place? | person? |

2 Which words or phrases make you want to read on?

3 a) Find an example of these types of sentences:
- A question
- A long, multi-clause sentence
- A short, snappy sentence.

b) Why has the writer used different types of sentences?

4 Re-read Extracts 2 and 3.

a) What are they about?

b) How does this link to the topic sentence in Extract 1?

2 Know how paragraphs are structured

> **Activity 4** **Understand how ideas are linked between paragraphs**

Key terms

Connectives
Words or phrases that link ideas together within and between sentences.

Pronouns
Words that are used to replace a noun. Writers use pronouns so that they do not repeat themselves too much. Pronouns also help them link their ideas and sentences together, for example: The **girl** guzzled her **drink**. **She** was in a hurry to finish **it**. In this sentence the pronoun 'she' replaces the noun 'girl'; the pronoun 'it' replaces the noun 'drink'.

Read this extract from an article which argues about the value of zoos.

Many people in our society are against them, yet there are so many positive aspects of zoos today. In fact, without them, many of these wild animals would be facing extinction. Many zoos run successful breeding programmes to help restore threatened species. This also means that far fewer animals we see in zoos now have been captured from the wild.

Although zoo animals are still not treated quite like guests in a posh hotel, their care has really improved. Zookeepers now understand that some animals need to do activities to stop them getting bored and to keep their brains working. This is why you'll often see monkeys playing with toys or lions 'hunting' for a meal.

As well as looking after captive animals, many zoos also contribute to the care of animals in the wild. London Zoo, for example has put more than £3 million towards projects in central Africa and Toledo Zoo in America is helping to repair some wild butterfly habitats.

Zoos also give scientists lots of opportunities to carry out research. Last year, zoos across the world took part in over 2000 research projects. The information they gather helps them develop new ways to look after animals and improve their health.

Beyond the positive impact on animals, zoos also affect the people visiting them. Zoos entertain and educate people with lots of information and activities for adults and children. They work hard to teach the public about different animals and about the importance of conservation.

Unit 3 Know how to understand presentation and organisation

1 a) Find the topic sentence in each paragraph.

b) What does each topic sentence tell you the paragraph will be about? Complete column 2 of the table.

c) What do you find out from the rest of each paragraph? Complete the table.

Paragraph	What the topic sentence tells me	What the rest of the paragraph tells me
1	Despite many people not liking them, there are lots of good points about zoos	Lists some of these good points such as breeding programmes
2		
3		
4		
5		

2 a) Find the connective at the start of paragraph 2.

b) Which statements on the right best describe why this connective has been used?

c) Find a connective from the start of each paragraph. Why have these connectives been used?

3 a) Find the pronoun 'them' in the first sentence. Does this pronoun refer to:
- zoos
- the people in our society?

b) Why has the writer used a pronoun here?

4 a) Find a pronoun in the topic sentence of paragraph 2.

b) To what does this pronoun refer?

c) Why has the writer used a pronoun here?

- All sentences have to begin with a connective.
- It links this paragraph with the one before.
- It adds another point to an argument.
- It shows a different side to an argument.

Activity 5 Understand how paragraphs structure a text

1 Which statement best describes how the piece is structured?
- The paragraphs alternate between for and against arguments for zoos.
- Each paragraph supports the point of view that zoos are good.
- Each paragraph supports the point of view that zoos are bad.
- Explain the reason for your answer.

Feedback
I can:
→ identify how writers link ideas within paragraphs
→ identify how writers link paragraphs together.

UNIT 4
Know how to write about texts

1 Know how to use quotations

Learning objective

I am learning to use quotations.

Key terms

Quotation
Exact words taken from somebody else's writing.

Quotation marks
Marks put around words to show that the words are a quotation: '…'.

When you are writing about a text, you often have to use the writer's words to explain something. This is called using a quotation. This section looks at how to use quotations in your writing.

Activity 1 — Understand what a quotation is

1 The quotation marks around the exact words in these sentences have been removed. Find the exact words that were said.

> The presenter on Soccer FM said that David Beckham was the greatest thing to happen to British football.
>
> Justin hopes that his next tour will take him to new and exciting places.
>
> Barack Obama's famous speech included the lines Yes we can!

2 Write out these sentences, adding quotation marks where they are needed.

> Weather experts are predicting 'slightly more unsettled, showery conditions' for next week.
>
> Alex Rider is described as having the body of an athlete.
>
> Mum said that I should grow up and start acting my age.

Unit 4 Know how to write about texts

Activity 2 — Use a quotation to make a point

Quotations can be used to help you make a point about a text. This is better than just using your own words as it shows that you have paid attention to the text. For example:

> The writer describes the sea as a 'hungry dog' to show how it was wild and noisy.

Read this short extract from the novel *Eragon*.

> Wind howled through the night, carrying a scent that would change the world. A tall Shade lifted his head and sniffed the air. He looked human except for his **crimson** hair and **maroon** eyes.

What do you know about ... *Eragon* by Christopher Paolini?
Eragon is a fantasy novel about dragons, elves and magic. A Shade is an evil sorcerer.

Expand your vocabulary
crimson – a deep pink-red colour
maroon – a deep purple-red colour

1 a) Answer this question using a quotation from the extract to complete the point.
What makes the Shade different from a human?

> The Shade is different from a human because his _____ make his appearance unusual.

b) Answer this question using a quotation from the extract. What was special about the scent being carried on the wind?

2 Check your writing.
Have you used:

- the writer's exact words?
- quotation marks to mark the quotation?

Feedback
I can:
→ use the exact words of the writer in quotations
→ use quotation marks to clearly mark quotations
→ use quotations to answer questions about a text.

2 Know how to choose good quotations

Learning objective

I am learning how to choose good quotations to help me explain something about a text.

When you write about a text, use quotations that really support the point you are making. Choose the quotations carefully so that they add to your point and are not too long.

Activity 1 — Use quotations that link to the point

The quotation you use in a response must link with the topic mentioned in your point.

Read this short passage from the novel *Artemis Fowl*.

> Sun did not suit Artemis. He did not look well in it. Long hours indoors in front of the monitor had **bleached** the glow from his skin. He was as white as a vampire and almost as **testy** in the light of day.

Key terms

Key words
Words in a question that tell you exactly what you should be thinking and writing about.

Topic word
A word or words in your first sentence that answer the question and set out what the paragraph will be about.

Expand your vocabulary

bleached – turned white
testy – grumpy

What do you know about … *Artemis Fowl* by Eoin Colfer?

Artemis Fowl is a science fiction, fantasy novel about a clever teenager called Artemis who sets out on a mission to uncover all the secrets of the fairy world.

1 a) Read this question and notice the key words.

What do we learn about Artemis from this extract?

b) Use the key words to write a point in answer to the question in your own words.

2 a) Read this student's point and notice the topic words.

> *From this extract we learn that Artemis does not like being outside.*

b) What are the topic words in this student's point?

Unit 4 Know how to write about texts

> From this extract we learn that Artemis does not go outside very often.

3 Complete each student's response by adding a quotation that links to the topic of each point.

> 'he was as white as a vampire'
> 'testy in the light of day'

| Activity 2 | Use quotations that add to the point |

The quotation you use must add something new to your point. The point should not just be the quotation written in your own words.

Read this student's response to the question:

> In this extract we learn that Artemis spends a lot of time in front of his computer, from the line 'Long hours indoors in front of the monitor'.

1 The point and quotation here are saying the same thing. Which words show this?

2 Complete the response with a quotation that adds to, rather than repeats, the point.

> We learn that Artemis spends a lot of time in front of his computer from the line _____.

> 'the monitor had bleached the glow from his skin'
> 'he was as white as a vampire'   'long hours indoors'

45

2 Know how to choose good quotations

> **Activity 3** | **Use short quotations**

You should try to avoid using really long quotations in your responses.

Read this further extract from *Artemis Fowl*.

Expand your vocabulary

- **adolescent** – teenager
- **authority** – power
- **gaunt** – skinny
- **mammoth** – enormous

> Artemis generally had that effect on people. A pale **adolescent** speaking with the **authority** and vocabulary of a powerful adult. Nguyen had heard the name Fowl before – who hadn't in the international underworld? – but he'd assumed he'd be dealing with Artemis Senior, not this boy. Though the word 'boy' hardly seemed to do this **gaunt** individual justice. And the giant, Butler. It was obvious that he could snap a man's backbone like a twig with those **mammoth** hands.

1 Find the key words in this question and use them to write a point. What do we learn about Butler from this extract?

2 a) Read this student's point and find the topic word.

> From this extract, we learn that Butler is quite a scary character.

b) The quotation this student has chosen to support his point is too long and wordy:

> From this extract, we learn that Butler is quite a scary character. I know this because it says that 'It was obvious that he could snap a man's backbone like a twig'.

- The quotation just repeats the point.
- The quotation is not written accurately.
- The quotation is too long.

Find a way to support the point efficiently.

Unit 4 Know how to write about texts

3 Now, answer this question using a brief quotation
What do we learn about Artemis from this extract?

Activity 4 | **Respond in detail to a text**

Read this extract from *Artemis Fowl*.

> Butler took the tiny **tome reverentially**. The bodyguard activated a compact digital camera and began photographing each wafer thin page of the Book. The process took several minutes. When he was finished, the entire volume was stored on the camera's chip. Artemis preferred not to take chances with information. Airport security equipment had been known to wipe many a vital disk. So he instructed his aide to transfer the file to his portable phone and from there email it to Fowl Manor in Dublin. Before the thirty minutes were up, the file containing every symbol in the Fairy Book was sitting safely in the Fowl server.

Expand your vocabulary
tome – book
reverentially – respectfully

1 a) Find the key words in this question. What must you write about? What do we learn about the setting of the story from this extract?

b) What clues can you find in the extract to help you answer the question?

2 a) Use the key words in the question and the information in the extract to write your point.

b) Support this point with a quotation.

3 Check your writing.
Have you:
- used a quotation that links to the point
- used a quotation that adds to the point
- used a brief quotation
- written the quotation accurately?

Feedback
I can:
→ choose quotations that best support my point
→ choose relevant and brief quotations.

47

3 Know how to write about a text

Learning objective

I am learning to write about texts in carefully constructed paragraphs.

Focus your effort

Use a PEE paragraph to show that you have read a text carefully and thought about the key ideas.

When you answer a question about a text, you will often need to write a detailed paragraph with a **point**, some **evidence** and an **explanation**. A good way to remember all of this is: PEE.

Activity 1 Understand PEE

What do you know about ... *Harry Potter and the Philosopher's Stone* by J. K. Rowling?

Harry Potter and the Philosopher's Stone is the first novel in the series of Harry Potter books. It is a fantasy novel about a boy named Harry who learns that he is a wizard and begins to discover a new and magical world.

1 Match the parts of PEE to the correct description.

1	Point	a)	A quotation from the text that supports the point
2	Evidence	b)	A sentence or two that explores and explains the effect of the quotation
3	Explanation	c)	A direct answer to the question

2 Read this extract from *Harry Potter and the Philosopher's Stone* and the question that follows.

> A pair of goblins bowed them through the silver doors and they were in a vast marble hall. About a hundred more goblins were sitting on high stools behind a long counter, scribbling in large **ledgers**, weighing coins in brass scales, examining precious stones through eyeglasses. There were too many doors to count leading off the hall, and yet more goblins were showing people in and out of these.

What impression do you get of the hall?

Expand your vocabulary

ledgers – notebooks

Unit 4 Know how to write about texts

3 Match each part of this student's answer to the correct part of the PEE paragraph.

1	Point	a)	I get the impression that the hall is very big.
2	Evidence	b)	This makes it seems like there must be hundreds of doors along the walls, and a room with hundreds of doors must be enormous.
3	Explanation	c)	I know this because it says 'There were too many doors to count leading off the hall'.

> **Key term**
>
> **Topic word**
> A word or words in your first sentence that answer the question and set out what the paragraph will be about.

Activity 2 Write a PEE paragraph

1 Read this further extract from *Harry Potter and the Philosopher's Stone*. It describes how Harry sees the Great Hall.

> It was lit by thousands and thousands of candles which were floating in mid-air over four long tables, where the rest of the students were sitting. The tables were laid with glittering gold plates and goblets. At the top of the hall was another long table where the teachers were sitting.
>
> The hundreds of faces staring at them looked like pale lanterns in the flickering candlelight. Dotted here and there among the students, the ghosts shone misty silver. Mainly to avoid all the staring eyes, Harry looked upwards and saw a velvety black ceiling dotted with stars.

a) Write your own PEE paragraph to answer the question:
What impression does the Great Hall make on Harry?

b) Label the point, evidence and explanation in your paragraph.

> **Feedback**
>
> I can:
> → include a point, evidence and explanation in my paragraphs
> → use connecting phrases
> → link my ideas by topic.

UNIT 5
Know how to uncover layers of meaning

1 Know how to read between the lines

Learning objective

I am learning to piece together information in a text and use it to understand what the writer is not telling me directly.

Focus your effort

Look carefully at the information the writer has given and use it to understand what they are not telling you directly. Use clues in the text to work things out.

Often, writers will not give readers all the details directly. Instead, they like readers to do some thinking and guessing for themselves. When you **read between the lines** you search for relevant information in a text and then draw conclusions about what must definitely be true about the character, place, situation and so on.

What do you know about … *Skellig* by David Almond?

Skellig is an award-winning children's novel by British author David Almond. It is narrated by a boy named Michael. His family move into a new house and he finds something very unusual while he is exploring there.

Activity 1 Find the information

1 Read this extract from *Skellig*.

> Something little and black scuttled across the floor. The door creaked and cracked for a moment before it was still. Dust poured through the torch beam. Something scratched and scratched in a corner. I tiptoed in and felt spider webs breaking on my brow.

Unit 5 Know how to uncover layers of meaning

2 Find all the clues that the writer gives you to build up information about this place.

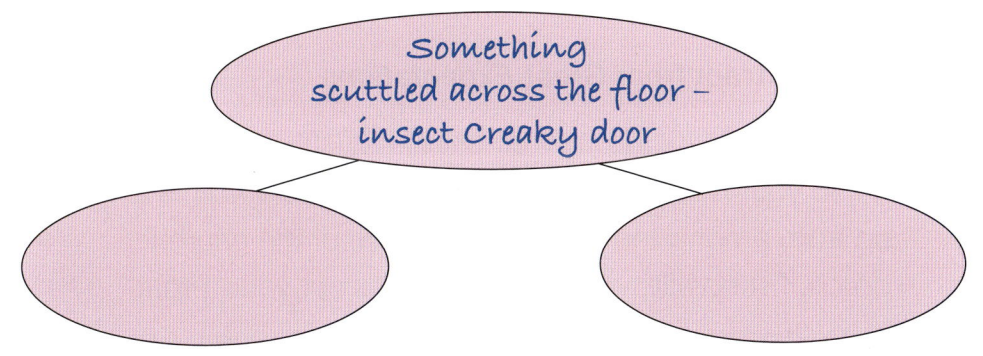

Something scuttled across the floor – insect Creaky door

3 What do these details suggest? From reading between the lines, what do you think this place is? Select from these possible answers:

| a forest | an attic | a classroom |
| a garage | a garden shed | a library |

4 Now, read the rest of the extract.

> Everything was packed in tight – ancient furniture, kitchen units, rolled up carpets, pipes and crates and planks. I kept ducking down under the hosepipes and ropes and kitbags that hung from the roof. More cobwebs snapped on my clothes and skin. The floor was broken and crumbly.

What new clues about this place does the writer give? For example:

- *Lots of things packed in – big objects like kitchen units*

5 What do these clues suggest? From reading between the lines, do you have a clearer idea about this place? Write three sentences to explain your ideas.

> *From the writer's description, I can deduce that this place is …*
> *I think this because …*
> *The words … also make me think …*

51

1 Know how to read between the lines

Activity 2 — Piece together the information

1 Read this extract from *Great Expectations*.

> "Hold your noise!" cried a terrible voice, as a man started up from among the graves at the side of the church porch. "Keep still, you little devil, or I'll cut your throat!"
>
> A fearful man, all in **coarse** grey, with a great **iron** on his leg. A man with no hat, and with broken shoes, and with an old rag tied round his head. A man who had been soaked in water, and smothered in mud, and **lamed** by stones, and cut by **flints**, and stung by nettles, and torn by briars.

Expand your vocabulary

- **coarse** – rough
- **iron** – old-fashioned term for chain
- **lamed** – damaged, so that walking is difficult
- **flints** – hard rocks

Unit 5 Know how to uncover layers of meaning

a) Find all the clues that the writer gives about this character. Add these to the table below.

Clues about the character	These suggest …
Terrible voice	A scary character
'I'll cut your throat'	The man is threatening and dangerous
Fearful	
Dressed in coarse grey	
Iron on his leg	

> **What do you know about … *Great Expectations* by Charles Dickens?**
>
> Charles Dickens was a great writer of the Victorian period. *Great Expectations* was first published in 1860 as monthly instalments in a magazine. It tells the story of an orphan, Pip, as he grows up and seeks his fortune in the world. The novel begins when Pip visits his parents' graves.

b) What does each detail suggest about the character? Add your thoughts to the table.

2 Piece all the information together. From reading between the lines, what type of person do you think this is?
Complete this paragraph to explain your ideas.

> I think this character is _____.
> I get this impression because the writer says _____ and _____. This makes me think he is _____ because _____.

Charles Dickens.

53

1 Know how to read between the lines

What do you know about ... *On Foot through Africa* by Ffyona Campbell?

Ffyona Campbell is a long-distance walker. She was the first woman to walk around the world. It took her over 11 years and she raised £180,000 for charity. She wrote three books about her experiences. *On Foot through Africa* is her account of walking from the bottom to the top of Africa.

Expand your vocabulary

contorted – bent
hacked – cut, chopped

Activity 3 Read between the lines to understand a text

1 Read this extract from *On Foot through Africa* by Ffyona Campbell.

> Soon afterwards I noticed that there were no footprints on the track. Where did the villagers walk? I left the road and 100 metres to the right, through thick bush, found a small track beside the remains of a railway. In places the metal line had been **contorted** by trees.
>
> Where the path had been worn to soft sand, the locals had **hacked** another one, giving themselves firm footing for at least another few years. Woodsmoke hung like mist around the trees and the light streaming through made me feel safe. It was too thick to be cooking fires and there was no sign of life until I heard the distant beat of drums.

2 Find these clues. What does each one suggest about the place and the people who live there?

 a) no footprints on the track

> *This clue suggests that the people do not like walking on the road. This might be because ...*

 b) worn to soft sand
 c) locals had hacked another one
 d) woodsmoke hung like mist around the trees

3 Find another piece of information about the smoke. What does this clue suggest?

4 Piece all the details together. From reading between the lines, what do you understand about this place and the people who live there?
Complete this paragraph to explain your ideas.

Unit 5 Know how to uncover layers of meaning

> From reading between the lines, I think that this place is ... I think this because ... The words ... also make me think ... The people that live there may ... I know this because ... The words ... also tell me ...

Activity 4   Read between the lines to make predictions

1 Read this extract from the novel *The Midnight Zoo* by Sonya Hartnett.

> But the bell had fallen from its height weeks ago, and now lay buried in silence beneath rubble; no small creature foraged in corners, because every scrap had already been carried away in beak and mouth and paw; and no villagers lay grumbling, for the people, like their bell, were gone. Their homes stood ruined, their beds broken into pieces, the bedroom walls slumped across the streets.

What do you know about ... *The Midnight Zoo*?

The Midnight Zoo is a novel by Sonya Hartnett, which won the Children's Book of the Year Award in Australia in 2011. It tells the story of two brothers in the time of World War II who come across an abandoned zoo with animals which can think, feel and talk like humans.

2 a) List the details about the village.

   b) What do these clues suggest?

3 From reading between the lines, what do you understand about this village?

Write a paragraph explaining your ideas. Use evidence from the extract.

4 Now, read this description of a character from the novel.

> The weeks he'd spent hiding in forests and sleeping in barns and wandering windswept roads had smudged dirt into his skin and dusted the colour from his clothes; probably he was hardly more visible than a shadow, but Tomas felt as brightly-lit as a shrine.

55

1 Know how to read between the lines

5 a) List the details about the boy.

b) What do these clues suggest?

6 From reading between the lines, what do you understand about Tomas?

Write a paragraph explaining your ideas. Use evidence from the extract.

7 Now, think about both of the extracts. How are the two linked?

Use the details and your ideas about each one to predict what this story is about.

What do you think has happened, is happening or is going to happen?

> I think that this is a story about _____.
> From reading between the lines in Extract 1,
> I understand that _____. This links to the
> second extract because _____. I predict
> that _____.

Key terms

Tone
The writer's attitude, thoughts or feelings.

Hyperbole
The use of exaggeration to create effect.

Activity 5 Understand tone

1 Read this review of a car, the Fiat Panda, from *Don't Stop Me Now* by Jeremy Clarkson.

> For reasons that aren't exactly clear, someone brought a new Fiat Panda round to my house to test. The cheapest version costs £6,295 and I wouldn't be at all surprised to find that Elton John spent more than that on his hair.
>
> I therefore wasn't expecting much. And to reinforce this view, I remember the old Fiat Panda well. Styled by someone who only had access to a ruler, it came with hammocks instead of seats, no interior trim and the top speed of a Galapagos turtle. It was fine for the walnut-faced peasantry of Italy but not really on for anywhere else.

Unit 5 Know how to uncover layers of meaning

2 **The writer uses hyperbole to describe the car. An example is:**

> 'I wouldn't be at all surprised to find that Elton John spends more than that on his hair.'

Here, the writer is emphasising how cheap the car is by saying that some people spend more on their hair!

   a) Find two more examples of hyperbole.

   b) What does each one suggest about the car?

   c) How does each one make the reader think and feel?

Hyperbole	What it suggests	Effect on reader
'I wouldn't be at all surprised to find that Elton John spends more than that on his hair.'	That the car is too cheap for a car.	Makes you think that the car must be no good or that it might break down easily.

3 **a)** What does the use of hyperbole tell us about the writer's feelings or attitude?

   b) What effect does the hyperbole have on the reader?

4 **From reading between the lines, explain what you understand about this text.**

Feedback

I can:

→ pick out the information a writer has given

→ piece the details together to read between the lines

→ read between the lines to better understand a text and make predictions.

57

2 Know how to read beyond the lines

Learning objective

I am learning to read beyond the lines to uncover the deeper meanings in a text.

Focus your effort

Pick out the details the writer has given you and piece them together to understand the text. Then dig a bit deeper by asking 'Well, why?' This will help you uncover further meanings in a text.

Reading 'beyond the lines' means that you can find the information that a writer has given you and use it to think about the deeper ideas that are not being said directly. These might be deeper meanings about people, places or even the writer's viewpoints.

Activity 1 Understand how to read beyond the lines

What do you know about … *Charlie and the Chocolate Factory*?

Charlie and the Chocolate Factory is a novel by the well-known children's author Roald Dahl. It is the story of Charlie Bucket, who finds a golden ticket in a Wonka bar and gets to visit the famous chocolate factory with his grandfather.

Read this extract from *Charlie and the Chocolate Factory* by Roald Dahl.

> The house wasn't nearly large enough for so many people, and life was extremely uncomfortable for them all. There were only two rooms in the place altogether, and there was only one bed.
>
> In the summertime, this wasn't too bad, but in the winter, freezing cold draughts blew across the floor all night long, and it was awful.

1 There are clues in the text to tell you that the family that lives here does not have a lot of money. What details tell you this?

- uncomfortable
- Only one bed

Unit 5 Know how to uncover layers of meaning

2 Now, dig a bit deeper and ask the question: 'Well, why?' Why are the family so poor? The text doesn't tell you this, so you have to make your own mind up. What might be possible explanations for why they are poor?

3 Dig even deeper. Ask: 'Well, why?' Why do they all carry on living together so uncomfortably? What more do you understand about the family now?

- -

Activity 2 — Piece together details

Read this extract from *Of Mice and Men* by John Steinbeck. It describes a woman who lives on a remote farm, with only her husband and the other farm workers for company.

> She had full, **rouged lips** and wide-spaced eyes, heavily made up. Her fingernails were red. Her hair hung in little rolled clusters, like sausages. She wore a cotton house dress and red **mules**, on the insteps of which were little **bouquets** of red ostrich feathers.

Expand your vocabulary

rouged lips – she's wearing red lipstick
mules – a slip-on shoe
bouquets – bunches

1 a) The information in the text tells you that the woman is very dressed up. What words or phrases tell you this?

b) Is the woman dressed properly for a farm? Explain your answer.

2 Now, dig a bit deeper. Ask: 'Well, why?' Why is the lady so dressed up on a farm in the middle of nowhere?

What possible ideas can you come up with? Do you agree with any of the ideas in the box?

| She's bored. | She likes fashion. | She wants attention. |
| She's lazy. | She's lonely. | She wants to go out. |

3 Dig even deeper. Ask: 'Well, why?' to some of your ideas from question 2. What more do you understand about her now?

What do you know about … *Of Mice and Men*?

Of Mice and Men is a novel by John Steinbeck which is set on a ranch in California, USA in the 1930s. The story follows two close friends – George and Lennie – over a week and we hear all about their hopes and dreams.

2 Know how to read beyond the lines

4 a) Which colour stands out in the description of the woman? Find evidence to support your answer.

b) What are the connotations of this colour? What does it make you think of?

c) Read further beyond the lines. Why has the writer chosen to use this colour? What does he want us to think about this character? What different ideas can you come up with? Do you agree with any of the ideas from the box?

> She is calm.   She is romantic.   She enjoys gardening.
> She is dangerous.   She is trying to attract attention.

d) Explain your thoughts.

> By using the colour _____ to describe the lady, the writer makes us think that she _____. I think this because the colour _____ reminds me of _____ which is also _____.

Key term
Connotation
An idea or feeling that a word makes you think of. 'Green', for example, has connotations of the environment and can make you feel calm.

Activity 3 Understand the writer's intentions

Read this extract from *On Foot through Africa*. It describes the people in a village that the writer passes through.

Key term
Writer's intentions
What the writer has purposefully said and done in a text to create a definite impression or reaction. This might link to how the writer feels, or how they want the reader to feel about something.

> I came behind them, white, undefended, feeling like a beetle walking into a dawn patrol of ants. An old man broke the silence with a barrage of shrill words. The crowd broke and re-formed around me, their shrill whooping getting louder and louder until it was a throbbing wall of sound. I daren't turn. I walked out of the village and I waved good-bye. Ten minutes later the hill behind was teeming with bands of children, whooping and hollering, their demands growing louder and louder.

Unit 5 Know how to uncover layers of meaning

1 Pick out at least three details that help you understand what the villagers were like.

2 Piece the details together. What is the writer suggesting about the villagers?

3 Now, dig deeper. Ask: 'Well, why?' Why did the villagers act like this? Write a sentence or two explaining your thoughts.

4 Dig even deeper to uncover the writer's intentions. Ask: 'Well, why?' Why has the writer described the villagers in this way? Think about:

   a) what the details suggest about her thoughts and feelings

   b) how the details make the reader feel and react.

5 Write a paragraph explaining your ideas. Use evidence from the extract.

> From reading beyond the lines in this text I can see that the writer felt _____. I can see this because it says _____ which suggests that _____. The writer also wanted the reader to feel _____. She did this by saying _____.

2 Know how to read beyond the lines

Activity 4 — Responding in detail

Read this extract from a Sherlock Holmes story 'The Adventure of the Speckled Band'.

What do you know about … Sherlock Holmes?

Sherlock Holmes is a very famous character created by Arthur Conan Doyle for a series of short stories in the 1880s. Sherlock Holmes is a very clever detective who solves lots of different mysteries with his friend Doctor Watson. The story 'The Adventure of the Speckled Band' is about a lady who asks Holmes to solve the mystery of her sister's death.

Expand your vocabulary

amid – amongst
hubbub – noise
blanched – made pale
writhed – twisted
convulsed – shaken

It was a wild night. The wind was howling outside, and the rain was beating and splashing against the windows. Suddenly, **amid** all the **hubbub** of the gale, there burst forth the wild scream of a terrified woman. I knew that it was my sister's voice. I sprang from my bed, wrapped a shawl round me, and rushed into the corridor. As I opened my door I seemed to hear a low whistle, such as my sister described, and a few moments later a clanging sound, as if a mass of metal had fallen. As I ran down the passage, my sister's door was unlocked, and revolved slowly upon its hinges. I stared at it horror-stricken, not knowing what was about to issue from it. By the light of the corridor-lamp I saw my sister appear at the opening, her face **blanched** with terror, her hands groping for help, her whole figure swaying to and fro like that of a drunkard. I ran to her and threw my arms round her, but at that moment her knees seemed to give way and she fell to the ground. She **writhed** as one who is in terrible pain, and her limbs were dreadfully **convulsed**.

Unit 5 Know how to uncover layers of meaning

1 a) Pick out all the details in the text about character (who), setting (where/when) and plot (what).

b) Use each detail to dig deeper. Ask: 'Well, why?'

c) Can you uncover any more layers of meaning?

Details	Dig deeper	Uncover layers of meaning
Wild scream	Something has scared her – there's someone in her room – she's been attacked	Someone's getting revenge on her for something – someone wants her money.
Clanging sound, mass of metal falling		

2 Be a detective. Write a short paragraph explaining what you think is happening and why.

3 a) Have a look at these descriptions. What do you notice about them?

> **wild** night   **wild** scream   **terrified** woman
>
> I stared at it **horror-stricken**

b) Think about the writer's intentions. Why might he have used these descriptions?
- What do they suggest about the narrator's thoughts and feelings?
- How do they make the reader react?

c) Find two more descriptions that add to this intention.

4 On the surface of this text, you see that a woman has been scared and hurt by something. What further understanding do you get when you dig deeper?
Write at least one paragraph about the deeper meanings in the text. Use evidence to support your ideas.

Feedback

I can:
→ dig deeper by asking 'Well, why?'
→ uncover different layers of meaning by digging even deeper
→ understand writers' intentions.

63

UNIT 6
Know how to understand points of view

1 Know how to identify fact and opinion

Learning objective

I am learning to:
- *understand the difference between a fact and an opinion*
- *find facts and opinions in a text*
- *understand why writers use facts and opinions.*

> **Key terms**
>
> **Fact**
> A piece of information that can be proven to be true, for example: Wimbledon is a tennis tournament.
>
> **Opinion**
> Someone's personal view. An opinion cannot be proven to be right or wrong, for example: Wimbledon is the best tennis tournament in the world.

Writers often use a mix of facts and opinion in their writing. In this section you will learn how to spot facts and opinions in texts and understand why they have been used by a writer.

Activity 1 — Understand fact and opinion

1 Read the following statements. Find the facts and the opinions.

a) If we don't stop global warming, all the polar bears will die.
b) Polar bears are an endangered species.
c) The album *Red* sold 1,208,000 copies the first week it was released in America.
d) Taylor Swift's latest album is her best.

Activity 2 — Find the facts

1 Read this text.

> The moon is the second brightest object in the sky. It moves around Earth and is our only natural satellite. It takes the moon about a month to orbit the Earth. The average distance from the Earth to the moon is 384,400 km.

Unit 6 Know how to understand points of view

2 List the facts in this text.

....

| Activity 3 | **Find the opinions** |

1 Read the text below.

> We've all dreamed of flying to the moon and seeing this remarkable orb up close. Now, thanks to the hard-working team at Lunar Launch, your dream will come true! Book your seat now for this once in a lifetime journey to the stars.

2 Find three opinions in the text.

....

| Activity 4 | **Understand why facts and opinions are used** |

1 Find the facts and opinions in this text on a bottle of shower gel.

ZING

Zing gives you the **most revitalising** shower experience! The invigorating oranges that make this **100% organic** shower gel are hand-picked from our beautiful Mediterranean orchards. Zing's pure orange oil is cold-pressed from the skins of the fruit and combined with other natural ingredients in this package of power! Showering with Zing will leave you fresh, smelling great and ready for anything!

2 a) What do the facts make you think about the shower gel?

b) What do the opinions make you think about the shower gel?

3 How do the facts and opinions work together to sell the shower gel?

Feedback

I can:
➡ find facts and opinions in a text
➡ understand why facts and opinions have been used.

65

2 Know how to comment on fact and opinion

Learning objective

I am learning to comment on the effect of facts and opinions in a text.

Writers use facts and opinions to help them achieve their purpose. In this section you will look at how facts and opinions work together in a text to have an impact on the reader.

Read this British Heart Foundation leaflet.

HELP US BEAT HEART DISEASE YOUR WAY. VOLUNTEER TODAY.

British Heart Foundation (BHF) volunteers tell us that helping the charity is not only incredibly rewarding, but also a lot of fun.

When you put your hand on your heart and join them, you too will be helping save and improve lives every year.

Despite huge advances, heart and circulatory disease remains Britain's biggest killer and our work is as vital as ever. We need as many of you as possible to join us and volunteer to help.

YOU'LL JOIN A GREAT TEAM
BHF volunteers are amazing! They helped raise over £25 million last year alone. When you join them you'll be part of a vibrant community active across the whole of the UK.

IT'S EASY AND FUN
You can choose how much time you want to give – it might be a regular day a week, or a few hours a year. You can be sure that whatever time you give will be a real help.

IT'S WHATEVER SUITS YOU
There are lots of ways to put your hand on your heart and volunteer. You could help with local fundraising activities, give time in a shop or put on a sponsored event with friends, to name just a few.

"Volunteering affects people's lives in a good way"
Lucky Omeke
BHF shop volunteer

Your first step
It's a small one – just call us to find out more on **0300 456 8353** (lines open Monday to Friday 9am – 5pm) or visit us at **bhf.org.uk/volunteer** anytime.

Alternatively, let us know how you would like to help by ticking one or more of the boxes overleaf. Then simply fill in your details and return the completed form to us in an envelope at the following freepost address:

FREEPOST British Heart Foundation (Volunteering)

Unit 6 Know how to understand points of view

Activity 1 | **Comment on facts and opinions**

Key terms

Fact
A piece of information that can be proven to be true, for example: Wimbledon is a tennis tournament.

Opinion
Someone's personal view. An opinion cannot be proven to be right or wrong, for example: Wimbledon is the best tennis tournament in the world.

1 a) Find this fact in the leaflet.

> They helped raise over £30 million last year alone.

Explain why this fact is used in the text. What effect does it have on the reader?

> *This fact makes me feel that volunteering can really make a difference because it helped to raise so much money …*

b) Find and comment on one other fact from the leaflet. What effect does it have on you?

2 a) Find this opinion in the leaflet.

> You'll join a great team

Explain why this opinion is used in the text. What effect does it have on the reader?

b) Find and comment on one other opinion. What effect does it have on the reader?

3 a) Read this sentence.

> heart and circulatory disease remains Britain's biggest killer and our work is as vital as ever

Identify the fact and the opinion. Notice how a fact and opinion have been used together. What is the effect of this?

b) Find one other sentence in the text that uses fact and opinion together. Comment on the effect.

Feedback

I can:
→ notice how facts and opinions work together in a text
→ comment in detail on the effect of facts and opinions.

67

3 Know how to identify and comment on points of view

Learning objective

I am learning to understand how writers use language to show their point of view.

Key terms

Exclamation
A sentence that is emphasised to show strong feelings.

Imagery
When one thing is compared to another to describe it.

Bias
When one side is favoured over another.

Texts often show a writer's **point of view** – this is what a writer thinks or feels about a particular topic. Sometimes a writer's point of view is obvious and sometimes it might be harder to spot.

Activity 1 Identify point of view

Read this text.

BENFICA NEED GOALS!

Fenerbahce edged Benfica 1-0 in the first leg of the other semi last week, so the Portuguese giants need some big displays from their star men in the second leg! Watch out for these heroes!

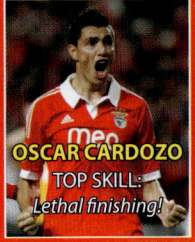

OSCAR CARDOZO — TOP SKILL: Lethal finishing!
NEMANJA MATIC — TOP SKILL: Bossing the midfield!
EDUARDO SALVIO — TOP SKILL: Electric pace!

WATCH IT! Benfica v Fenerbahce Thursday, May 2 ITV4 ★ 8.05 pm

1 Complete this passage to explain the writer's point of view. Use these words in the box to the left to answer:

talented
goals
'top'
good
work

> The writer thinks that Benfica is a _____ team. It has lots of _____ players with _____ skills. However, they need to _____ hard to score some _____ in their next game.

2 a) Find an example of each of these language and presentation features.

b) Explain how each feature shows the writer's point of view.

Unit 6 Know how to understand points of view

| Activity 2 | Comment on how writers show point of view |

1 **Find the verb 'edged'. It makes it seem like the other team only just managed to score a goal.**
How does this word add to the writer's point of view?

2 **The writer uses the word 'heroes' to describe the players. This is an example of imagery.**
Find these three other examples of imagery:

- giants
- lethal finishing
- electric pace

How does this imagery add to the writer's point of view?

3 **How do the pictures in the text add to the writer's point of view?**

Focus your effort

Identify the techniques a writer has used to show their point of view – look for the types of words and sentences used and how they have been presented. Think about how these techniques influence the way the reader thinks too.

| Activity 3 | Understand bias |

Read this technology blog.

> So, you want to buy a new phone but which way are you going to go? Out-dated Android? Or stylish Apple? The sleek design of the latest iPhone is a clear winner for me – it's shiny, light and slim; the new HTC however is large and clunky. But what about usability? The iPhone 5 is intuitive, it's fast and almost graceful. The Nexus is slow in comparison and no-where near as user-friendly. Plus, there's all the great accessories you can get for Apple products! If you ask me, Android need to work much harder if they're to keep up with this clear market superstar …

1 **List the words used to describe each phone.**

2 **Complete this passage to explain which phone the writer is biased towards.**

69

3 Know how to identify and comment on points of view

> The writer is biased towards _____. In their point of view it is the best phone. I know this because the text uses words like _____. On the other hand, the writer thinks that _____ is not as good. The text uses words like _____ which makes it seem _____.

Key terms

Pronoun
A word used in place of a noun.

Personal pronouns
Include 'I', 'me' and 'you'.

Superlatives
Words that tell us one thing is greater than another, for example: she had the *longest* hair. He was the *most* intelligent in his class.

Activity 4 — Understand how writers influence your point of view

Read this review of the 'Top 3 Christmas Movies'.

After the family has finished playing charades and all that's left on the table is the bones of the turkey, you'll need some movies you can all snuggle up on the couch to enjoy …

1. THE GRINCH

In this twisted world, that explores all camera angles, everyone wears strange turned-up noses and fears the big green monster – the Grinch. The Grinch is one of the biggest Christmas icons, which is ironic since he hates Christmas and tries to do everything to ruin it. It's a magical Christmas movie, and if you haven't watched it already, I don't know where you've been!

Unit 6 Know how to understand points of view

2. HOME ALONE: LOST IN NEW YORK

Why the parents leave a 10-year-old boy home alone again? We don't know. How he makes all his mechanical traps? We're oblivious. All we know is that Kevin McCallister is the cutest, most cunning boy alive. So when New York's criminals escape prison and stupidly come after him again, they're in for a treat. This is an instalment of one of the most hilarious family franchises of all time.

3. LOVE ACTUALLY

Is the most perfect romantic seasonal movie ever. Starring the best of British, Hugh Grant, who brings his awkward humour to the table and Colin Firth who just delivers his all-round awkwardness! In this film everyone's got someone, and it's the best film to snuggle up to your partner with.

1 a) The writer uses the second person pronoun 'you' in the introduction. Find another example of a second person pronoun.

b) Find an example of a first person pronoun.

c) What is the effect of first and second person pronouns?

2 a) Find an example of each of these techniques:
- Superlatives
- Facts
- Exclamations

b) What is the effect of each of these techniques?

3 Put all your ideas together in a paragraph.
- Write a sentence explaining the writer's point of view.
- Write a sentence or two about a language feature the writer has used to show this point of view. Consider the effect this has on the reader.
- Write a sentence or two about a language feature the writer has used to influence the reader's point of view. Consider the effect this has on the reader.

Feedback

I can:
→ identify a writer's point of view
→ understand how language has been used to show point of view
→ understand how language has been used to influence point of view.

UNIT 7
Know how to comment on language

1 Know how to comment on the effect of words in a text

Learning objective

I am learning to:
- identify effective words in a text
- comment on the effect of words.

Focus your effort

Identify the different types of words used by a writer and then comment on the effect they create.

Writers make careful decisions about what words to use to have an impact on the reader. This section will help you identify the types of words a writer has used and think about the effect they create.

Activity 1 Understand different types of word classes

1 Match the word class to the correct definition.

Word class		Definition
1 noun	a)	a word to describe a noun
2 adjective	b)	a word that expresses an action, a state or a happening
3 verb	c)	an object or thing
4 adverb	d)	a word to describe a verb

2 Read this short extract from *The Truth about Verity Sparks* by Susan Green.

> Feeling pretty pleased with myself, I trotted along happily until I heard my name called. It was a girl's voice. She was halfway down a lane, standing in the shadows, a small skinny creature with a cloud of yellow hair.

Unit 7 Know how to comment on language

Find one example of each of the following:

a) Noun

b) Adjective

c) Verb

d) Adverb

| Activity 2 | Find and comment on how writers use words effectively |

Read this extract. It is taken from a retelling of a Greek myth.

> Like a hawk, Perseus swooped out of the sky. But the serpent reared up out of the water and tossed him against the cliff. Perseus' shield fell from his shoulder, the helmet and bag fell from his grasp. He drew his sword and leapt between the princess and the monster's open mouth, and drove his sword into the beast's shoulder.

1 a) Find five words that are effective in showing what happens.

 b) What class of words are they?

2 Choose three words from the extract above. Write a sentence explaining why each word is effective. Here is an example:

> I think the verb 'swooped' is an effective word because it makes it sound like Perseus is moving really fast. It adds excitement to the passage.

1 Know how to comment on the effect of words in a text

> **Activity 3** **Compare the effect of words**

Read these extracts from Lemony Snicket's *A Series of Unfortunate Events: The Bad Beginning*.

What do you know about … *A Series of Unfortunate Events: The Bad Beginning*?

A Series of Unfortunate Events: The Bad Beginning is the first novel in a series by Lemony Snicket. The story follows three young orphans and all the strange – and often-dangerous – people and places they encounter.

Expand your vocabulary

assortment – lots of different types
dilapidated – falling to pieces

Extract 1

The Baudelaire children looked out and saw the prettiest house on the block. The bricks had been cleaned very well, and through the wide and open windows one could see an **assortment** of well-groomed plants. Standing in the doorway, with her hand on the shiny brass doorknob, was an older woman, smartly dressed, who was smiling at the children.

Extract 2

The children looked from the well-scrubbed house of Justice Strauss to the **dilapidated** one next door. The bricks were stained with soot and grime. There were two small windows, which were closed with the shades drawn even though it was a nice day. Rising above the windows was a tall and dirty tower that tilted slightly to the left. The front door needed to be repainted, and carved in the middle of it was an image of an eye. The entire building sagged to the side, like a crooked tooth.

1 a) Find three effective words in each extract.

  b) What types of words are they?

  c) What does each word make you think about each house and its owner? How does each word make you feel?

Add your thoughts to the 'effect' column of the table.

Unit 7 Know how to comment on language

Extract	Words	Word class	Effect
1	prettiest	adjective	Makes it seem like the house is attractive; it would be a nice place to live.
	shiny		
2	stained		

2 Complete this paragraph to compare the use of words in the extracts. Use these words to help you:

dislike   comfortable   disgusted   negative
positive   attracted   prettiest   different   stained

The writer's choice of words shows us how _____ the two houses are. Words such as _____ in the first extract create a very _____ description so we feel _____ towards the house and think that we would be _____ there. The second extract is much more _____. Words such as _____ make us _____ the house and maybe even feel _____ about what might be inside.

Feedback

I can:

→ identify nouns, adjectives, verbs and adverbs
→ comment on the effect of a writer's choice of words.

2 Know how to comment on sentences in a text

Learning objective

I am learning to understand why writers use different sentence types and lengths.

This section looks at how sentences can vary by type and length. Writers use a range of different sentences to create impact and effect.

Key term

Sentence
- A group of words that is complete and can stand on its own
- Usually contains a verb and obeys grammar rules
- Begins with a capital letter and ends with a full stop
- There are four types of sentence: command, statement, question, exclamation.

Activity 1 Understand different sentence purposes

1 Match each sentence with the correct definition and example.

1	Command	a)	A sentence that wants an answer	i)	I enjoyed the film last night.
2	Statement	b)	A sentence that tells you something	ii)	How are you feeling?
3	Question	c)	A sentence that gives an order	iii)	What an awesome goal!
4	Exclamation	d)	A sentence that expresses emphasis or strong feelings	iv)	Put the fire on.

2 Read this extract.

> He watched the clock tick its seconds slowly. Why didn't the bell ring? He was dying to get out into the fresh air.
>
> Brrrrrriiiinnnnng! Yes, at last!
>
> 'Chairs up.' Everyone scrambled from their seats.

Unit 7 Know how to comment on language

a) Find an example of each sentence purpose below.

b) Complete the table to explain the effect of each sentence purpose. Use the explanations on the right.

Sentence purpose	Example	Effect
Statement		
	Yes, at last!	
Command		

Tells the reader exactly what is happening.

Helps the reader feel his frustration because we don't know the answer either.

Shows the reader that he is feeling excited. Makes the reader feel happy too.

Shows that the teacher is in charge.

Activity 2 Understand different sentence lengths

Read these two extracts.

Extract A

The air was full of sound, a deafening and confusing conflict of noises: the clangorous din of the Martians, the crash of the falling houses, the thud of the trees, fences, sheds flashing into flame, and the crackling and roaring of fire.

Extract B

My head whirls.

Cancer is bad.

Cancer is really bad.

People die from cancer.

Dom might die.

My best mate might die.

2 Know how to comment on sentences in a text

1 **How are the sentences different in each extract?**

2 a) Which words describe the sentence length in Extract A?

| short | detailed | punchy | powerful |
| long | descriptive | dramatic | flowing |

b) Which words describe the sentence length in Extract B?

3 Write a short paragraph about the sentence length in each extract.

> In Extract A the sentence is _____ and _____. I think this helps to make the extract _____ because _____.

Activity 3 — Comment on sentences

Focus your effort

Identify the different types and lengths of sentences a writer has used. Then consider and comment on the effect that is created by these sentences.

What do you know about ... *Holes*?

Holes is a novel by Louis Sachar. It tells the story of Stanley who is sent away to a camp for bad boys. The campers are forced to dig a hole every day in a dried-up lake bed, in the hot sun.

1 a) Read this extract from *Holes*. Notice the different kinds of sentences the writer has used.

> Here's a good rule to remember about rattlesnakes and scorpions: If you don't bother them, they won't bother you.
>
> Usually.
>
> Being bitten by a scorpion or even a rattlesnake is not the worst thing that can happen to you. You won't die.
>
> Usually.
>
> Sometimes a camper will try to be bitten by a scorpion, or even a small rattlesnake. Then he will get to spend a day or two recovering in his tent, instead of having to dig a hole out on the lake.
>
> But you don't want to be bitten by a yellow-spotted lizard. That's the worst thing that can happen to you. You will die a slow and painful death.
>
> Always.

b) Write a short paragraph about the effect of the sentences used.

Unit 7 Know how to comment on language

2 a) Read this extract from an article, 'Dawn of the Dumb', by the journalist Charlie Brooker. Notice what sentences the writer has used.

> It's a mystery to me. If the whole point of fashion is to distinguish yourself from the herd, why queue up to be part of it? Am I missing something here? I suspect not. But then I don't 'get' fashion. I once went out with a girl who was obsessed with dressing up; a real clothes nerd. While we were together, she developed a serious jeans habit. Each week, a new pair. She'd bring them home and show them to me, bubbling with excitement.

b) Write a paragraph about the effect of the sentences used.

Feedback

I can:
- identify different sentence types and lengths
- comment on the effect of different sentences.

3 Know how to comment on imagery

Learning objective

I am learning to:
→ *identify different types of imagery in a text*
→ *comment on the effect created.*

Focus your effort

Identify the imagery used by a writer, label it with the correct term and comment on the effect created.

Imagery is created when writers describe one thing by comparing it to another. Imagery allows writers to use words to create pictures and feelings in the mind of the reader.

Activity 1 Understand imagery

1 Match each technique to the correct definition and example.

1 Simile	a) When one thing is said to be another	i) His schoolbooks felt like heavy rocks on his back.
2 Metaphor	b) When something that is not human is given human qualities	ii) The chair swallowed him up.
3 Personification	c) When one thing is compared to another using the words 'as', 'like' or 'than'	iii) A wave of people flooded over him.

2 Read this short extract.

> A bright sun smiled down, warming the silver sand with its touch. For a second, the beach lay still, like a smooth blanket. But in the distance, excited chatter of children could be heard: the peace was about to be invaded.

a) Find an example of each technique.

b) Add a comment about each technique to the table.
- What is each technique being used to describe?
- What does it help you picture in your mind?

Technique	Example	Comment
Simile		
	the peace was about to be invaded.	

Unit 7 Know how to comment on language

Activity 2 | **Comment on imagery**

Read these descriptions of the island from *Lord of the Flies*.

All round him the long scar smashed into the jungle was a bath of heat. He was **clambering** heavily among the creepers and broken trunks when a bird, a vision of red and yellow, flashed upwards with a witch-like cry; and this cry was echoed by another.

The shore was **fledged** with palm trees. These stood or leaned or **reclined** against the light and their green feathers were a hundred feet up in the air.

But the island ran true to form and the incredible pool, which clearly was only invaded by the sea at high tide, was so deep at one end as to be dark green. Ralph inspected the whole thirty yards carefully and then plunged in. The water was warmer than his blood and he might have been swimming in a huge bath.

Ralph did a surface dive and swam under water with his eyes open; the sandy edge of the pool loomed up like a hillside. He turned over, holding his nose, and a golden light danced and shattered just over his face.

What do you know about ... *Lord of the Flies*?

Lord of the Flies is a novel by William Golding about a group of schoolboys who find themselves stranded on a desert island after their plane crashes.

Expand your vocabulary

clambering – climbing
fledged – covered (originally meaning covered with feathers as in a young bird)
reclined – rested

1 a) Find two similes.
- A witch-like cry
- …

b) Find two metaphors.

c) Find two examples of personification.

81

3 Know how to comment on imagery

2 a) Complete this paragraph to comment on the use of similes.

> The writer uses the simile _____ to describe _____. This gives the impression that _____. It makes me feel _____ because _____.

b) Write a paragraph about the writer's use of metaphor.

c) Write a paragraph about the use of personification.

What do you know about … 'The Highwayman'?

'The Highwayman' is a narrative poem by Alfred Noyes, written in 1906. A highwayman is a robber from the eighteenth century who steals from travellers on the road. This opening stanza describes the highwayman riding his horse through the night.

Expand your vocabulary

torrent – flood
galleon – an old-fashioned ship
moor – land, countryside

dark	happy
bright	stormy
day-time	spooky
night-time	scary

Activity 3 Explain the effect of imagery

Read the opening to the poem 'The Highwayman' by Alfred Noyes.

> The wind was a **torrent** of darkness among the gusty trees,
> The moon was a ghostly **galleon** tossed upon cloudy seas,
> The road was a ribbon of moonlight over the purple **moor**,
> And the highwayman came riding—
>   Riding—riding—
> The highwayman came riding, up to the old inn-door.

1 a) Choose some of the words from the purple box to describe the setting and atmosphere.

b) Find some imagery that the writer has used to help the reader understand the setting and atmosphere.

2 Read this student's response to the setting of the poem.

> The poem is set at night. I know this because the writer says that the 'moon was a ghostly galleon'. This tells me it is night-time because the moon is out and the writer's use of simile also creates quite a spooky atmosphere.

Unit 7 Know how to comment on language

3 a) Read the teacher's comments to this student.

Check:
- Has the student found an example of imagery?
- Is it labelled it correctly?
- Is the effect of the imagery explained?

> You have commented well on the effect of the imagery.
>
> However, 'The moon was a ghostly galleon' is not a simile.
>
> Re-write your paragraph making sure you label the imagery correctly.
>
> Add one more sentence explaining how the example of imagery makes you feel as a reader.

b) Re-write the student's paragraph making the improvements that the teacher has suggested.

4 a) Now, write your own PEE paragraph (see p.44) about the setting of the poem.
- Make a **point** about the setting of the poem.
- Find some **evidence** (a quote) to support your point.
- **Explain** what imagery the writer has used in this quote and comment on the effect it has on you as a reader.

b) Check:
- Have you found an example of imagery?
- Have you labelled it correctly?
- Have you explained the effect of the imagery?

Feedback

I can:
→ identify different types of imagery in a text
→ comment on the effect created
→ structure my thoughts into a paragraph.

4 Know how to comment on rhetorical devices

Learning objective

I am learning to find rhetorical devices in a text and comment on their effect.

Focus your effort

Use your scanning skills to find and identify the rhetorical devices used by a writer, label them with the correct term and comment on the effect created.

Rhetoric is language that has a powerful effect on an audience. It is often used to persuade a reader or listener. Rhetorical devices are the different techniques that are used to create this powerful effect. In this section, you will look at extracts from two rhetorical speeches.

Activity 1 Understand rhetorical devices

1 Match each rhetorical device with the correct definition.

Rhetorical device	Definition
1 Rhetorical questions	a) Words or phrases that describe an emotion or make an audience feel an emotion
2 Emotive language	b) An exaggerated or 'over the top' description, for example: this book weighs a ton
3 Lists of three	c) When a word or phrase is repeated once or more
4 Hyperbole	d) A question that does not need an answer. It is asked to make an audience think about an idea or issue.
5 Repetition	e) When things are listed in groups of three

2 Read this extract from Old Major's speech to the animals in *Animal Farm*.

Now, **comrades**, what is the nature of this life of ours? Let us face it: our lives are miserable, **laborious**, and short. We are born, we are given just so much food as will keep the breath in our bodies, and those of us who are capable of it are forced to work to the last atom of our strength; and the very instant that our usefulness has come to an end we are slaughtered with **hideous** cruelty. No animal in England knows the meaning of happiness or leisure after he is a year old. No animal in England is free. The life of an animal is misery and slavery: that is the plain truth.

Unit 7 Know how to comment on language

Match each highlighted example to the correct rhetorical device.

Rhetorical device	Example
Rhetorical question	
Emotive language	
List of three	
Hyperbole	
Repetition	

> **What do you know about … Animal Farm?**
>
> *Animal Farm* is a novel written by George Orwell in 1944. It tells the story of a group of farm animals who decide to stand up for themselves after being inspired by a speech from Old Major, a pig. They take over the farm and drive the farmer away because they hope it will give them a better life.

Activity 2 Consider the effect of rhetorical devices

Think about the effect, or impact, of Old Major's choice of words on his audience. What is he trying to do? Find and comment on his use of rhetorical language. Read the next paragraph from Old Major's speech.

Expand your vocabulary

comrades – friends
laborious – hard work
abundance – more than enough
hideous – extremely horrible, terrible

> But is this simply part of the order of nature? Is it because this land of ours is so poor that it cannot afford a decent life to those who dwell upon it? No, comrades, a thousand times no! The soil of England is fertile, its climate is good, it is capable of affording food in **abundance** to an enormously greater number of animals than now inhabit it. This single farm of ours would support a dozen horses, twenty cows, hundreds of sheep – and all of them living in a comfort and a dignity that are now almost beyond our imagining. Why then do we continue in this miserable condition?

1 Find these three rhetorical devices in the extract. What effect does each have?

Rhetorical device	Example	Effect
Rhetorical question		

2 How does each device make the:
- animals feel
- reader feel?

85

4 Know how to comment on rhetorical devices

Activity 3 — **Comment on a range of rhetorical devices**

Read this extract from a speech by President Obama.

What do you know about … Barack Obama?

Barack Obama became the President of the USA in 2009. He gave a speech to the country when he was voted in as President. In this extract from the speech, he talks about a 106-year-old lady he met and all the changes she has seen in America in her life.

Expand your vocabulary

creed – belief
ballot – voting card
tyranny – cruel use of power
democracy – a country where the people choose their leaders by voting

And tonight, I think about all that she's seen throughout her century in America – the heartache and the hope; the struggle and the progress; the times we were told that we can't, and the people who pressed on with that American **creed**: Yes we can.

At a time when women's voices were silenced and their hopes dismissed, she lived to see them stand up and speak out and reach for the **ballot**. Yes we can.

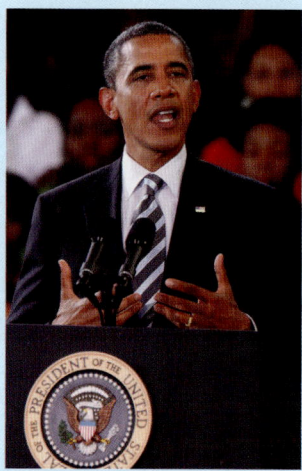

When there was despair in the dust bowl and depression across the land, she saw a nation conquer fear itself with a New Deal, new jobs and a new sense of common purpose. Yes we can.

When the bombs fell on our harbor and **tyranny** threatened the world, she was there to witness a generation rise to greatness and a **democracy** was saved. Yes we can.

She was there for the buses in Montgomery, the hoses in Birmingham, a bridge in Selma, and a preacher from Atlanta who told a people that 'We Shall Overcome.' Yes we can.

A man touched down on the moon, a wall came down in Berlin, a world was connected by our own science and imagination. And this year, in this election, she touched her finger to a screen, and cast her vote, because after 106 years in America, through the best of times and the darkest of hours, she knows how America can change. Yes we can.

Unit 7 Know how to comment on language

1 **Find examples of these rhetorical devices:**
- Emotive language
- Lists of three
- Repetition

2 **The writer also uses contrasts as a rhetorical device.**

a) Here are two examples:

> the heartache and the hope
>
> the struggle and the progress

> **Key term**
>
> **Contrast**
> When two opposite things or ideas are mentioned together.

b) Explain the effect of the contrast: 'the heartache and the hope'.

3 **Look at how the writer uses the pronouns 'I' and 'we'. Explain the effect of these pronouns.**

4 **Answer this question:**
How does the speech have a powerful effect on the audience?

a) Write a PEE paragraph (see p.44) about emotive language.

> The speech uses lots of emotive language, for example _____. All of these words make the audience _____. It makes them feel _____.

b) Now, write a PEE paragraph about the use of contrasts.

c) Write one more PEE paragraph about another rhetorical device from the speech.

Feedback

I can:
→ identify rhetorical devices in a text
→ comment on their effect.

87

UNIT 8
Know how to share a response to a text

1 Know how to read a text aloud

Learning objective

I am learning to know how to read a text aloud to bring out its meaning.

Reading a text aloud is a useful way to help you understand it better. When you read aloud it can help to think about how to say different words to bring the meaning out.

Focus your effort

Vary your *pace, volume* and *emphasis* to bring a text to life when you read it aloud. Using tactics like this will also make reading more fun and entertaining for you and anyone listening to you!

| Activity 1 | Look for clues in a text |

Read this extract from the poem 'Blood Brothers' by Willy Russell.

> I wish I was our Sammy
> Our Sammy's nearly ten.
> He's got two worms and a catapult
> An' he's built an underground den.
> But I'm not allowed to go in there,
> I have to stay near the gate,
> 'Cos me Mam says I'm only seven,
> But I'm not, I'm nearly eight!

Focus your effort

When you read poetry, make pauses at punctuation marks, not at the end of a line.

1 Notice what punctuation has been used. How does punctuation influence the way we read things out loud?

1	Full stop	a)	Signals that a short pause is needed.
2	Comma	b)	Marks the end of a sentence. Signals that the sentence needs to be emphasised to show emotion.
3	Exclamation mark	c)	Marks the end of the sentence. A pause is needed.

2 Read the poem aloud. Use the punctuation clues to help you.

Unit 8 Know how to share a response to a text

3 Look at the final line. What emotion could the exclamation mark signal? Read the line as if you are:
- excited
- angry
- whining.

4 Read the first two lines aloud.
  a) Emphasise the word:
  - wish
  - ten.

  b) Try different volumes. c) Try different speeds. d) Try adding pauses.

  How does each thing change the meaning?

5 a) How do you think the narrator feels about his older brother?

  b) Read the rest of the poem aloud. Experiment with emphasis, volume, speed and pauses to show the narrator's feelings.

> He looks up to him.
> He's angry with him.
> He's jealous of him.

Activity 2 — Make a text interesting to hear

Read this student's opening to a presentation about fear.

> The thing I am most scared of is snakes. I hate the way they slither along. I hate the hissing noise they make. But most of all I hate how dangerous they are. Yes, there are plenty of harmless snakes out there but I'd rather be on the safe side and steer clear of them all just in case.

1 Read it aloud. Notice what clues the punctuation gives you.

2 How could this student read the presentation aloud to make it more interesting to listen to?

Make notes to show:
- which words could be emphasised
- what speed should be used
- what volume should be used
- where pauses could be added.

> The thing I am *most* scared of is snakes. I *hate* the way they slither along. I *hate* the hissing noise they make.

- emphasise
- pause
- emphasise

3 Read the paragraph aloud. Use your notes to make it interesting to listen to.

1 Know how to read a text aloud

What do you know about … *Private Peaceful*?

Private Peaceful is a novel by Michael Morpurgo. It is narrated by a boy called Thomas Peaceful. He tells the story of his life and his time in the trenches during the First World War. This extract is about a gas attack that Thomas experiences.

Activity 3 — Bring a text to life

Read this passage from *Private Peaceful* by Michael Morpurgo.

> The gas is only feet away now. In a moment it will be on me, around me, in me. I crouch down hiding my face between my knees, hands over my helmet, praying it will float over my head, over the top of the trench and seek out someone else. But it does not. It's all around me. I tell myself I will not breathe, I must not breathe. Through a yellow mist I see the trench filling up with it. It drifts into the dugouts, snaking into every nook and cranny, looking for me. It wants to seek us all out, to kill us all, every one of us. Still I do not breathe. I see men running, staggering, falling. I hear Pete shouting out for me. Then he's grabbing me and we run. I have to breathe now. I can't run without breathing. Half-blinded by my mask I trip and fall, crashing my head against the trench wall, knocking myself half-senseless. My gas mask has come off. I pull it down, but I have breathed in and know already it's too late. My eyes are stinging. My lungs are burning. I am coughing, retching, choking. I don't care where I am running as long as it's away from the gas.

1 **Read the passage aloud. Notice what clues the punctuation gives you.**

2 a) Make notes on:
- what is happening in the passage
- how the is narrator feeling.

b) Find evidence to support your ideas.

c) Make notes on how you might read parts of the passage aloud.

Unit 8 Know how to share a response to a text

		Evidence	Reading aloud notes
What is happening?	Gas attack	Gas is only feet away now	Emphasise 'feet'
	Gas has got into the trenches	Snaking into every nook and cranny	
	Soldiers trying to run away		
How is the narrator feeling?	Scared		

3 Read the passage aloud. Use your notes to bring it to life.

Activity 4 Read aloud on the spot

1 Read this passage from *Private Peaceful*. Notice the punctuation, the emotion, the atmosphere and what is happening.

> **Expand your vocabulary**
> **Hun** – an insulting word used to describe German soldiers during the First World War

> At last I'm in the reserve trench and it is clear of gas. I'm out of it. I wrench off my mask, gasping for good air. Then I am on my hands and knees, vomiting violently. When at last the worst is over I look up through blurred and weeping eyes. A **Hun** in a mask is standing over me, his rifle aimed at my head. I have no rifle. It is the end.

2 Read the passage aloud. Make quick decisions on emphasis, volume, speed and pauses.

3 What changes would you make if you were to read the passage aloud again?

> If I were to read the passage aloud again, I would slow down more towards the end to show that …

Feedback
I can:
→ vary my emphasis, volume, speed and pauses when reading aloud
→ make quick choices about how to read aloud to bring out meaning and emotion.

2 Know how to write an essay about a text

Learning objective *I am learning to write an essay in response to a text.*

You will often be asked to write an essay about a text you have read. This section looks at drawing all your reading skills together to help you write in detail about a text.

Activity 1 — Understand the question

Read this extract from *Private Peaceful*.

> The gas is only feet away now. In a moment it will be on me, around me, in me. I crouch down hiding my face between my knees, hands over my helmet, praying it will float over my head, over the top of the trench and seek out someone else. But it does not. It's all around me. I tell myself I will not breathe, I must not breathe. Through a yellow mist I see the trench filling up with it. It drifts into the dugouts, snaking into every nook and cranny, looking for me. It wants to seek us all out, to kill us all, every one of us. Still I do not breathe. I see men running, staggering, falling. I hear Pete shouting out for me. Then he's grabbing me and we run. I have to breathe now. I can't run without breathing. Half-blinded by my mask I trip and fall, crashing my head against the trench wall, knocking myself half-senseless. My gas mask has come off. I pull it down, but I have breathed in and know already it's too late. My eyes are stinging. My lungs are burning. I am coughing, retching, choking. I don't care where I am running as long as it's away from the gas. At last I'm in the reserve trench and it is clear of gas. I'm out of it. I wrench off my mask, gasping for good air. Then I am on my hands and knees, vomiting violently. When at last the worst is over I look up through blurred and weeping eyes. A Hun in a mask is standing over me, his rifle aimed at my head. I have no rifle. It is the end.

Unit 8 Know how to share a response to a text

1 **Write a brief summary of what the text is about.**

2 **a)** Read this essay question, noting the key words.
   How does **the writer** use **language** and **structure** to **engage the reader**?

   b) You are being asked to write about **how the writer engages the reader**. What does the question ask you to focus on? Choose your answers from the box on the right.

   > I must talk about _____ and _____.
   > Language is the _____ used and structure is the way they are _____ into _____ and _____.

   | paragraphs |
   | structure |
   | organised |
   | words |
   | sentences |
   | language |

Activity 2 — Make notes

1 **Read the extract again, looking for interesting language features:**
   - Powerful verbs
   - Personification

2 **Scan read the text for interesting structure features:**
   - Short, punchy sentences
   - Repetition

3 **a)** Choose two to three things from each list that you want to write about.

Writer's techniques	Evidence	Effect
Effective use of verbs		
Personification		
Short punchy sentences		

   b) Find some evidence to support each technique.

   c) Make notes on how that technique/quote hooks the reader – what effect does it have on you?

2 Know how to write an essay about a text

Activity 3 Pull your ideas together

1 Have you:
- read the extract ☐
- identified the writer's techniques ☐
- found evidence ☐
- made notes on the effect on the reader? ☐

2 You are now ready to write your essay. Remind yourself of the question:
How does the writer use language and structure to engage the reader?

3 Choose one technique from your table to write up as a PEE paragraph.

> To hook the reader, the writer uses _____.
> An example of this is _____. This hooks the reader because _____. It makes me feel like _____.

4 Have you:
- written a **point** which talks about the writer's technique ☐
- included a quotation as **evidence** of that technique ☐
- **explained** how that technique/quote hooks the reader? ☐

5 Now, choose another technique from your table to write about. Remember to write about both language and structure.

6 Do your two paragraphs link well together? Choose one of these connectives to begin paragraph 2:
- Furthermore
- Also
- Secondly
- In addition

Unit 8 Know how to share a re...

Activity 4 — Make improvements

1 Read this student's response to the essay question.

> To hook the reader, the writer uses repetition. An example of this is 'on me, around me, in me'. The repetition of the word 'me' makes me focus on the narrator and what is happening to him. It makes me want to read on to find out if he's okay.
>
> Furthermore, the writer uses verbs to hook the reader. For example, 'running, staggering, falling'. The verbs help me to picture clearly what is happening and I want to read on to find out what will happen next.

Check:

Can you find the point, evidence and explanations? ☐

Do both paragraphs answer the question? ☐

Are the paragraphs well linked? ☐

2 Now, read the teacher's feedback to this student.

> These are two good PEE paragraphs! You have found good techniques and quotations.
>
> Try to say something other than 'it makes me want to read on' in your explanations. Think really carefully about what effect that technique has – why has the writer used it? How does it make you feel as a reader?
>
> Re-write the second PEE paragraph with a more thoughtful explanation.

3 Re-write the student's second PEE paragraph, taking note of the teacher's comments.

4 Now, finish off your own essay response. You must write four to six paragraphs in total.

5 Check:

Do all your paragraphs answer the question? ☐

Have you written about language **and** structure? ☐

Have you included point, evidence and explanation in each paragraph? ☐

Are your paragraphs linked? ☐

Feedback

I can write an essay that:
→ is detailed
→ is structured
→ backs up the points I make with evidence.

95

Know how to write sentences to interest your reader

1 Know about different types of sentence

Learning objective

I am learning about how sentences can be built up using clauses.

Key terms

Clause
A group of words containing key elements such as a verb.

Sentence
A group of words that may consist of a single clause or may contain several clauses held together by subordination or coordination.

Sentences are made from groups of words called clauses. A single-clause sentence has just one main clause. For example:

> John ate chocolates.

There are two types of multi-clause sentence. A sentence may have more than one main clause, held together by **coordination**.

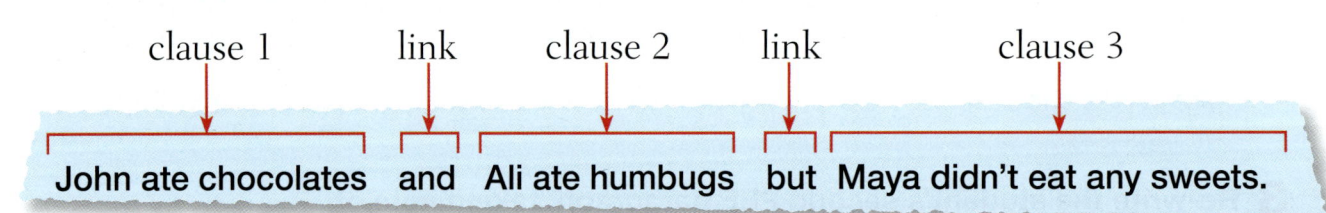

clause 1	link	clause 2	link	clause 3
John ate chocolates	and	Ali ate humbugs	but	Maya didn't eat any sweets.

A sentence may have a main clause and one or more **subordinate clauses** that depend on it. The subordinate clauses are always joined with a connective.

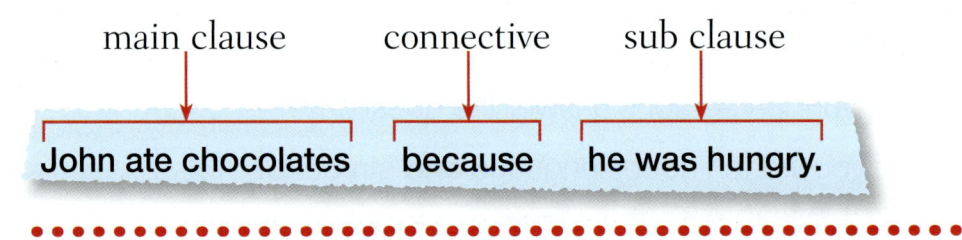

main clause	connective	sub clause
John ate chocolates	because	he was hungry.

Unit 9 Know how to write sentences to interest your reader

Activity 1 — Explore single-clause sentences

A common pattern for a single-clause sentence is:

subject + verb + object + adverbial

Subject	Verb	Object	Adverbial
John	ate	chocolates	greedily

Here are boxes of subjects, objects, verbs and adverbials. Using the pattern above, pick words from the boxes to make five different sentences. The sentences can be as crazy as you like as long as they follow the grammatical pattern.

Subject	Object	Verb	Adverbial
elephants	phones	find	secretly
bananas	glass	break	loudly
children	walls	eat	in the jungle
potatoes	leaves	kiss	after dinner
televisions	tractors	paint	rapidly
trees	dolls	tickle	angrily
fish	jewellery	like	on the table
mountains	swords	destroy	under the ground

For example:

Elephants kiss tractors after dinner.

Notice that you can put the adverbial at the front of the sentence if you like:

After dinner elephants kiss tractors.

1 Know about different types of sentence

> **Activity 2** — Explore sentences with clauses held together by coordination

Certain connectives called *conjunctions* can be used to link clauses using coordination.

The connectives in these sentences are: *and, but, or.*

> Kazuo went to the zoo **and** he saw a tiger.
>
> Kazuo went to the zoo **but** he didn't see a tiger.
>
> Every day Kazuo went to the zoo **or** he went to the museum.

In all these sentences two main clauses are linked with the conjunction.

Sentences with coordinated clauses can be extended as much as you like:

> Kazuo went to the zoo and he saw a tiger, and he saw a zebra, and he saw a crocodile and …

(You could add every animal in the zoo and make a very long sentence.)

You wouldn't *want* to write like this though.

Write three sentences using these patterns of coordinated clauses.

_____, and _____.

_____, but _____.

_____, or _____.

Unit 9 Know how to write sentences to interest your reader

Activity 3 — Explore sentences with clauses held together by subordination

Connectives can be used to make one or more clauses in the sentence dependent on the main clause. We can group these connectives according to their meaning:

Time	Place	Reason	Purpose
after	where	because	to
as	wherever	since	in order to
before		for	
since		as	
till			
until			
when			
while			

Here is a common pattern for linking subordinated clauses in sentences:

Main clause	Connective	Subordinate clause
Jo laughed	when	he read the comic.

Choose four connectives – one from each column of the first table – and write four sentences using this pattern.

Notice that sometimes you can change these sentences around so the subordinate clause comes first.

Feedback

I can:
- understand the difference between single-clause and multi-clause sentences
- use connectives to write sentences that link clauses through coordination
- use connectives to write sentences that link clauses through subordination.

2 Know how to use and vary single-clause sentences

Learning objective

I am learning how to use single-clause sentences effectively.

Key term

Adverbial
The part of a sentence that gives extra information about what is happening – such as when it happened or how it happened.

Single-clause sentences are very effective for:
- stating information clearly
- creating effects in a story.

The basic pattern for a single-clause sentence is:

Subject	Verb	Object
The girl	cooked	pasta.

You can say more about the subject and object by adding adjectives.

| The *new* girl | cooked | *delicious* pasta. |

You can say more about what happened by adding one or more adverbials.

adverbial | | | | adverbial

| Yesterday, | the new girl | cooked | delicious pasta | very quickly. |

Notice how the adverbials can go at the start or the end of the sentence or in both places.

every day
without stopping
last week
carelessly
like wild beasts
quickly
tearfully
in silence
under the shed

Activity 1 — Build and vary single-clause sentences

Using patterns like the ones shown, build up these single-clause sentences by adding adverbials. Use your own ideas or choose from the adverbials box. Vary where you place the adverbials.

- The family watched the film.
- She sent about 40 texts.
- We dug a large hole.

Unit 9 Know how to write sentences to interest your reader

Activity 2 Use single-clause sentences for clarity

Look at this short paragraph about badgers. It is written in single-clause sentences so the information is presented clearly.

> Badgers belong to the weasel family. They grow to 90 centimetres in length. Badgers eat earthworms, insects and grubs. For digging, badgers have short, strong legs. Over short distances they can run at nearly 20 miles per hour.

1 Write a similar short paragraph about another animal presenting the facts in clear, single-clause sentences. Try to vary the sentences by not always starting with the subject.

Activity 3 Use single-clause sentences in a story

Look at this extract from a story. The writer has used short simple single-clause sentences in places for two reasons:
- For emphasis – to make more impact.
- To make the action more dramatic.

> Unwillingly, the two boys entered the old warehouse because the dog just had to be in there. It might have hurt itself or it could be trapped in some way. The old warehouse was deeply scary. Rusting steel beams had collapsed in places leaving sheets of crumbling, toxic asbestos ready to crash down on anyone below.
>
> Suddenly all hell broke loose. Bloodcurdling screams split the air. From above, stones came crashing down. Flames belched from a hole in the floor.
>
> The boys froze in terror.

1 Identify the short, simple single-clause sentences and decide what effect they are designed to have on the reader.

2 Write a similar extract from a story where you include some short, simple single-clause sentences.

Feedback

I can:
- → vary simple single-clause sentences by placing adverbials
- → use simple single-clause sentences to state factual information clearly
- → use simple single-clause sentences to create effects in a story.

101

3 How to write sentences using subordination

Learning objective

I am learning to write sentences using subordination in order to express:

→ *time and place*
→ *a condition or a concession*
→ *a reason.*

> **Key term**
>
> **Connective**
> A word that links the main clause and the sub clause. These words are also called conjunctions.

A sentence held together by subordination has a main clause and one or more subordinate clauses that depend on it. The clauses are always joined with a connective.

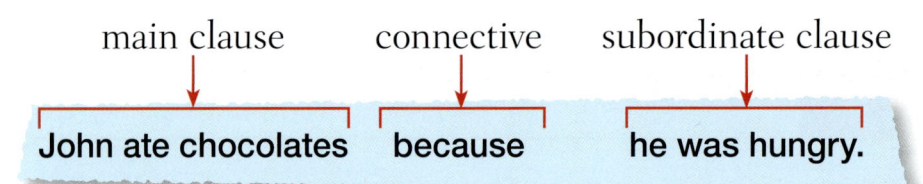

main clause	connective	subordinate clause
John ate chocolates	because	he was hungry.

This is a sentence where the subordinate clause expresses a reason. The writer has used a subordination to tell us not just that John ate chocolates but why.

Writers use subordination in sentences to express more than one idea. The key to writing sentences using subordination is using a range of connectives.

Writers can vary their sentences by placing the subordinate clause before the main clause. Notice the use of a comma to separate the two clauses.

> Because he was hungry, John ate chocolates.

Activity 1 — Express time

Some of the connectives that are used to express time are:

> after   as   before   since
> until   when   while

Use this main clause and each of the connectives to write seven sentences by adding a subordinate clause.

> I climbed out of bed.

For example:

> After the alarm rang, I climbed out of bed.

Activity 2 — Express a condition or a concession

Some of the connectives used to express a condition are:

> if
> unless

Some of the connectives used to express a concession are:

> although
> though

Look at the way these connectives are used in this poem.

103

3 How to write sentences using subordination

Argument

Although I shouted,

I am still your friend.

Although I called you names,

I am still your friend.

Although I walked away,

I am still your friend.

If I say sorry,

Will you forgive me?

Unless you forgive me,

You are not my friend.

Write your own poem based around these connectives using a similar pattern.

You could use a topic such as Winning. The poem might start:

Although the pitch was muddy,
We won the football game.

Activity 3 — Express a reason

Some of the connectives used to express a reason are:

because   since   as

Write five sentences giving reasons for things Shirley did. Use all three connectives. Vary your sentences by sometimes putting the subordinate clause first.

Action	Reason
Got up early	Had to catch a train
Shirley got up early because she had to catch a train.	
Took an umbrella with her	It might rain
Arrived at the station early	Had to buy a ticket
Became very impatient	There was a long queue
Had to go back to the ticket office	Had left her umbrella
Only just caught the train	Was waiting on the wrong platform

Activity 4: Explore longer multi-clause sentences using subordination

Sentences can have more than one subordinate clause. For example:

After I went to the match, I was happy because we won.

In this sentence there are two subordinate clauses – one expresses the time and one the reason for being happy.

Use your own ideas to complete these sentences:

When I _____, I _____ because _____.
Although we _____, we _____ before _____.
If you _____, you can _____ until _____.

Feedback

I can:
- use subordination in sentences for different purposes
- use a range of connectives to link subordinated clauses in sentences.

4 Improve your style by varying your sentences

Learning objective

I am learning to vary the way I write sentences through:
- fronting
- changing the order of clauses.

> **Key term**
>
> **Fronting**
> Moving a part of the sentence that might normally come later to the beginning.

Many sentences start with the subject and the verb and, if they are sentences using subordination, with the main clause.

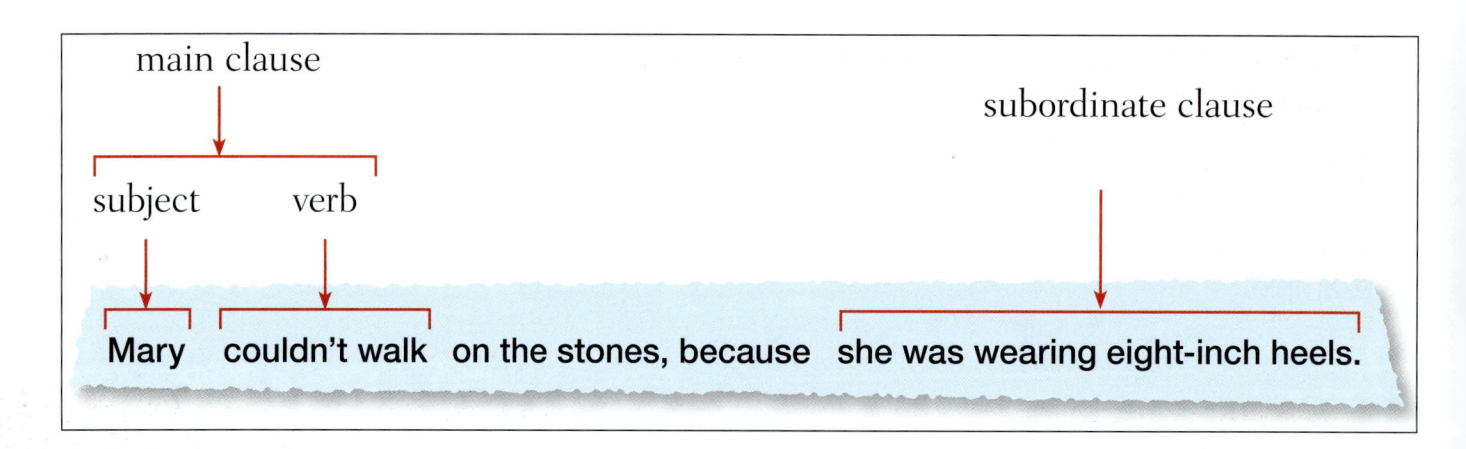

```
        main clause                              subordinate clause
      ┌─────┴─────┐                           ┌─────────┴─────────┐
   subject    verb                                       │
      │         │                                        │
    Mary   couldn't walk   on the stones, because   she was wearing eight-inch heels.
```

This is a good, clear sentence but good writers don't build every sentence in the same way. Readers like some variety in sentences as it adds interest. You can also vary your sentences to achieve certain effects, such as to build tension in a story, or to explain a complex idea.

You can vary your sentences by:
- moving parts of the main clause in front of the subject (fronting)
- putting the subordinate clause before the main clause
- dropping a subordinate clause inside a main clause.

Activity 1 — Vary single-clause sentences

1 Vary these single-clause sentences by moving part of the sentence to the front.

- The helicopter crashed over the sea yesterday.
- He became gradually addicted to shopping on the internet from the age of sixteen.
- The thief drove away at speed after the robbery.
- The smell of a brand new car is attractive to most people for a while.
- A graffiti artist had painted the train in bright colours along the side during the night.

2 Does moving parts of the sentence around change the meaning in any way?

Activity 2 — Vary multi-clause sentences

1 Vary these sentences by changing the order of the clauses.

- Nothing worked properly because the car was so old.
- The game had to be stopped whenever it rained because the surface became too slippery.
- I will come to your house if you want me to, although it is a long way.
- The cruiser docked at the space station after it had travelled for two light years, although there was an alien virus on board.
- Di almost fainted when she saw Richard because he was so good-looking.

2 How has varying the sentences changed the meaning?

4 Improve your style by varying your sentences

Activity 3 Use a mix of sentences

Look at this piece of writing describing a famous painting. All the sentences have been built in the same way. It's your job to spice it up. Re-write it varying the sentences. Use a mix of types of sentences and vary the position of parts of your sentences. Add some of your own sentences if you wish.

> It was a clear night. You could not see the moon. The stars were out. The stars lit up the deep blue sky. Lights shone in the buildings by the river. The buildings were silhouettes. The lights sparkled on the river. The lights were yellow and orange against the dark blue water. You could hear music from a cafe. It was a guitar with violin. Some small boats were moored nearby. They floated as if asleep. Little waves slapped against the sides of the boats. Shortly the church clock would strike twelve times for midnight. Then what would happen?

Activity 4 **Use embedded clauses**

An embedded clause is one that is put inside another one.
For example:

> The friends decided to keep walking although they were tired.
>
> The friends, although they were tired, decided to keep walking.

subordinate clause embedded in main clause

Notice that you have to use two commas to embed a clause.
Change these sentences by embedding the subordinate clause.

- The cattle grew fat because the grass was lush.
- The soldiers were invisible to the enemy after they had camouflaged themselves.
- Many people think that the Earth's climate will change, if we keep burning fossil fuels.
- The referee's decision was completely wrong many people thought.

● ●

Feedback

I can:

→ change a sentence by moving parts of it around

→ improve a piece of writing by adding variety to the sentences.

UNIT 10 Know how to use punctuation to make your meaning clear

1 Know how to punctuate sentence boundaries

Learning objective

I am learning to identify the ends of sentences and use punctuation to mark these.

In writing, a sentence is a group of words that
- is complete and can stand on its own
- usually contains a verb and obeys grammar rules
- begins with a capital letter and ends with a full stop.

So, 'Very boy terribly went.' is not a sentence because it does not obey grammar rules.

'Is too hot.' is grammatical but feels incomplete so is not a proper sentence.

In writing you mark the beginning of a sentence with a capital letter.

We mark the end of a sentence with a full stop.

If it is a question you use a question mark.

If it is an exclamation you use an exclamation mark.

Activity 1 — Identify sentences

Which of these groups of words are full sentences and which are not?

- Going not tomorrow.
- As he flew across America.
- The book was already open at the right page.
- Why I thought felt very some go yes yes do!
- During the night.
- Go to the top of the road.
- Have you thought about it?
- Ow, that really hurt!
- Although the flowers were beautiful.
- Broken bottles, empty tins, old shoes.

Unit 10 Know how to use punctuation to make your meaning clear

Activity 2 — Mark sentence boundaries

If you forget to mark our sentence boundaries with capital letters and full stops, your writing becomes confusing and difficult to read. The writers of these two texts forgot about sentence boundaries. Add capital letters and full stops for them.

> My mum is great she is a really good cook her chips are always crispy she never forgets things and always keeps her promises she doesn't mind driving me to my friends her jokes are quite good but dad doesn't think so.
>
> On Saturday we built a guinea pig mansion we made it out of scrap wood my dad got it from his friend when it was finished we put the guinea pigs in they loved it they ran in and out of the rooms there is a ramp so they can go upstairs no cats or foxes can get in and eat them.

Activity 3 — Use questions and exclamations

All these sentences end with full stops but some should end with question marks or exclamation marks. Correct the sentences.

- Help, I'm drowning.
- He shouted, 'No I won't.'
- The bus was a single-decker.
- Do you fancy a drink.
- What do you think of that new track.
- I went home as soon as I could.
- I've found it at last.
- Why do volcanoes erupt.
- What a joke.
- Is it a plane or a UFO.

Feedback

I can:
- identify when a group of words is a sentence
- mark sentence boundaries correctly
- use question marks and exclamation marks.

2 Know how to use commas to make your meaning clear

Learning objective

I am learning to use commas:
➡ *to mark the boundary between main and subordinate clauses*
➡ *with fronted adverbials*
➡ *to show embedded clauses and phrases*
➡ *so that my sentences are clear to the reader.*

The comma is a little mark that is easy to forget when you are writing but sentences can be very confusing without them. For example:

> Some of the time travellers think about home.

Is this a sentence about time travellers? Or should it read like this?

> Some of the time, travellers think about home.

To use commas correctly, remember these rules:

- Use commas to mark the boundary between a main and a subordinate clause.

    Because it had started to rain, she decided to take the bus home.

- Use a comma after a fronted adverbial as it makes the meaning clearer.

    After rain, coats need to dry.

- Use commas at the beginning and end of embedded clauses and phrases.

    Mobiles, particularly smart phones, are very popular with young people.

- You don't need a comma if you use a conjunction to connect two main clauses.

    I tried to build the wardrobe myself but I gave up in despair after five hours.

Unit 10 Know how to use punctuation to make your meaning clear

Activity 1 Use commas to mark clause boundaries

Use commas to mark the clause boundaries and make these sentences easier to read and understand.

- Although the sun was shining Daisy began to shiver because the wind was icy and because she had forgotten her coat.
- To find the treasure go to the park park in the car park find the waste-bin and dig underneath it until you hit a big stone covering the treasure chest.

Activity 2 Use commas with fronted adverbials

1 Use commas after the fronted adverbials where it will make the sentence clearer and easier to understand.

- After eating Goldilocks went to sleep in Baby Bear's bed.
- In a rush Jamil tripped and banged his head.
- Like a stampeding herd the children rushed into the dining room.

2 Write three of your own sentences with fronted adverbials, using a comma if needed.

Activity 3 Use commas with embedded clauses and phrases

1 Embed the clauses and phrases into the sentences remembering to use commas.

- The old warplane flew overhead. (which was one of the last of its kind)
- The picture was a forgery. (in fact)
- The dragon flapped its wings and flew. (with a roar and a puff of smoke)

2 Write three sentences of your own with embedded clauses or phrases and mark the boundaries with commas.

Feedback

I can use commas:
→ to mark sentence boundaries
→ with fronted adverbials
→ to embed phrases.

3 Know how to write lists

Learning objective

I am learning how to punctuate lists using:
- *commas*
- *bullet points.*

When you write a list you need to use punctuation correctly so you don't confuse the reader. Look at this headline from a magazine:

> **JOANNE TAKES PLEASURE IN COOKING HER FAMILY AND HER DOG**

You would be less worried about Joanne if the headline had a comma:

> **JOANNE TAKES PLEASURE IN COOKING, HER FAMILY AND HER DOG**

> Rule 1: Use commas to separate items in a list. We do not normally put a comma before the word 'and' in a list.

Bullet point lists can be punctuated in different ways. You will practise two of the most common ways in this section.

Unit 10 Know how to use punctuation to make your meaning clear

Format A

In the afternoons students enjoy playing: — *Colon to start the list*
- Hockey or football on the school field. — *Full stops*
- Swimming in the pool.
- Badminton in the gym. — *Capital letters*

or Format B

In the afternoons students enjoy playing: — *Colon to start the list*
- hockey or football on the school field — *No capitals or full stops*
- swimming in the pool
- badminton in the gym

Rule 2: Be consistent with your punctuation when you are using bullet points. Don't mix up the two formats.

Activity 1 Use commas in lists

Complete the verses in this list poem, using the same pattern and remembering the commas.

On sunny days:

Water glints, shadows appear, coats come off and skin browns.

On rainy days:

_____

On frosty days:

_____

On snowy days:

_____

3 Know how to write lists

Activity 2 — **Use bullet points for short item lists**

Use Format B for lists with short items. For example:

> The most useful hand tools for a gardener are:
> - spade
> - fork
> - hoe
> - trowel
> - rake

1 Write your own bullet list of things to take on a long train journey to stop being bored.

> To avoid being bored on the train take:

2 Write a bullet list of your own recommending snack foods or sweets.

Activity 3 — **Use bullet points for longer item lists**

Use Format A for lists with longer items. For example:

> To be good at punctuation you must remember to:
> - Put capital letters at the start of sentences.
> - Place full stops, question marks and exclamation marks at the end of sentences.
> - Use commas within the sentence to make it clearer and easier to read.

116

Unit 10 Know how to use punctuation to make your meaning clear

1 Write your own bullet list of some rules for staying safe on the way home from school.

> To stay safe on the way home from school:

2 Write a bullet list of your own giving advice on a topic that interests you. For example:

> Important things to remember when keeping a hamster are:

Feedback

I can:
→ use commas in lists in my own writing
→ punctuate bullet points consistently in my own writing.

4 Know how to use impact punctuation

Learning objective

I am learning how to use punctuation to make an impact on my reader.

Key term

Emphasis
Expressing something strongly to show the reader it is important.

Three main ways to put **emphasis** on part of a sentence are to:
- place it at the start of a sentence
- place it at the end of the sentence after a pause
- repeat it.

Using the correct punctuation is important to make this work. In addition, exclamation marks can be used to give whole sentences more emphasis.

Here are some examples:
- *Snails, he actually ate snails.*
  Notice the comma that has to go between the emphasised word and the rest of the sentence.
- *She had committed the most vile form of murder: poisoning.*
  Notice you put a colon between the emphasised word and the rest of the sentence to signal that an explanation or illustration is coming.
- *The test was ever so, ever so difficult.*
  Notice you put a comma between the repeated elements.
- *He drove the wrong way up a one-way street. What a dangerous piece of driving!*
  The exclamation mark helps to add emphasis.

Activity 1 Add punctuation for impact

Look at these sentences. The part the author wanted to emphasise has been highlighted. Add the punctuation (commas, colons, exclamation marks) needed in the sentences.

Unit 10 Know how to use punctuation to make your meaning clear

- '**No reason** there is no reason for it,' he muttered.
- At the end of a terrible season the manager could only expect one thing **the sack**.
- What he did was **very very wrong**.
- '**What talent**' shouted the spectator.
- Now she saw exactly what had caused it **a broken promise**.
- **Empty** the treasure chest was empty.
- The jail door was open and the prisoners were **gone gone gone.**
- **Chris** he was the real hero, not Joe.
- She had dyed her hair purple and green. **How tasteful**
- There was just one thing he loved about school **art lessons**.

Activity 2   Re-write to add emphasis

Re-write these sentences to add emphasis. Use punctuation to help create the effect.

- She loved anything made of gold. (emphasise gold)
- The summer was very wet. (emphasise how wet it was)
- He cooked home-made burgers. They were delicious. (emphasise how delicious they were)
- They all thought that the holiday was a success. (emphasise success)

Activity 3   Give your own writing emphasis

Make up some of your own sentences in which you use punctuation to help give emphasis.

1. **Write a sentence in which you put a word you want to emphasise at the start.**
2. **Write a sentence in which you use a colon to emphasise the last part.**
3. **Write a sentence in which you use repetition to emphasise something.**
4. **Write a sentence in which you use an exclamation mark to add emphasis.**

Feedback

I can:

→ use commas to punctuate for emphasis

→ use colons to punctuate for emphasis

→ use exclamation marks to punctuate for emphasis.

UNIT 11
Know how to use paragraphs to organise your writing

1 Know how to use topic sentences

Learning objective

I am learning how to:
- *write better paragraphs*
- *use topic sentences to introduce a paragraph.*

Key terms

Topic sentence
A sentence, often near the start of a paragraph, which identifies the main focus of that paragraph.

Paragraph
A section of a piece of writing. A new paragraph marks a change of topic focus, or a change of time. or, in dialogue, a change of speaker.

A paragraph is a section of a piece of writing. A new paragraph marks a change of topic, or a change of time.

To write a good paragraph you need to be clear about the aspect of the topic you are going to write about. Writers often use the first sentence to show the reader which aspect they are focusing on. This sentence is called a topic sentence.

For example, in an article about the killing of rhinos for their horns a paragraph on the different equipment used by the criminal gangs might begin with this topic sentence.

> Criminal gangs use a range of high tech equipment and weapons to kill rhinos and avoid detection.

From this sentence the reader knows that the rest of the paragraph will give more detail about what the rhino poachers use: things such as night vision scopes, silenced weapons, darting equipment and helicopters.

Unit 11 Know how to use paragraphs to organise your writing

Activity 1 — Choosing topic sentences

Look at this article on rhino poaching.

Choose the correct topic sentence from the sentence bank on the next page for the start of each paragraph.

A _____ Hundreds of rhinos are killed every year and the number goes up and up. For example in South Africa, where most surviving rhinos live, 122 were killed in 2009 but over 300 have been killed in every year since then.

B _____ Rhino horns have become extremely valuable because in Asia many people believe that the horn can cure a range of illnesses. The horns are ground into a fine powder and made into tablets. There is, however, no medical proof that rhino horn works as a medicine.

C _____ They use helicopters with night vision equipment to hunt the rhinos at night. They have powerful rifles with silencers.

D _____ Firstly, don't buy any rhino horn products. Secondly, tell your friends about the problem. Thirdly, you could make a donation to one of the charities which provides funds to help fight the poachers.

121

1 Know how to use topic sentences

Topic sentences

1. There are three things you can do to help.
2. Rhinos are large mammals.
3. Rhino poaching is threatening to kill off all the rhinos in Africa.
4. Rhinos are killed for their horns.
5. People like to see rhinos in safari parks.
6. Because the trade in rhino horn is so profitable, the criminal gangs of poachers are well equipped and difficult to catch.

Activity 2 **Writing topic sentences**

Think of and then write topic sentences for these paragraphs.

You are what you eat

_____ By changing your diet you can reduce the risk of being ill. Heart disease, diabetes and some forms of cancer have proven links to what people eat. Of course, obesity (being over-weight) is also a major health risk.

_____ Most fruits and vegetables are part of a heart-healthy diet. They are good sources of fibre, vitamins, and minerals. Eat low-fat breads, cereals, crackers, rice, pasta, and starchy vegetables (such as peas, potatoes, and corn). These foods are high in the B vitamins, iron and fibre. They are also low in fat. Grain products, including whole grains are also highly recommended.

Unit 11 Know how to use paragraphs to organise your writing

_____ Protein foods that are recommended are:

- meat
- poultry
- seafood
- dried peas
- lentils
- nuts
- eggs

_____ Eat no more than six cooked ounces of meat, poultry, and fish daily. Also, avoid duck, goose, marbled meats (such as a ribeye steak), organ meats such as kidneys and liver, and prepared meats such as sausage, and hot dogs.

_____ For example:

maintain your ideal body weight

eat less than 2,400 mg of salt per day

limit the amount of alcohol you drink

Feedback

I can:

→ understand what a topic sentence is

→ understand how to use a topic sentence.

123

2 Paragraphs and connectives

Learning objective

I am learning how to:
→ write better paragraphs
→ use connectives to link paragraphs.

Good writers lead their readers through what they write by making clear links between one paragraph and another. Look at this example. The connecting words and phrases that make the links are in bold.

> CDs are becoming less and less popular as a way of enjoying music. In 2012 the number of CDs sold went down by about a fifth. In the last five years sales are down by nearly a half.
>
> **One reason for this** is that more and more music fans are buying music through downloads. Digital downloads from sites such as iTunes were up by 15 per cent in 2012.
>
> **But in spite of** this increase in digital sales, album sales overall were still down. So is this bad news for the music industry?
>
> **The answer** is yes and no. It is **bad news** for record shops on the high street which are selling less even though they have brought down prices. The **good news** for musicians is that digital downloads of singles have soared to a record high.
>
> **Another reason** for the decline in sales of recorded music is that more and more fans choose to listen to music streamed from internet sites such as Spotify. So does this mean musicians will be out of pocket and music will die out?
>
> **Probably not because, fortunately**, musicians do receive a fee when their music is streamed. **Furthermore**, streaming is not always possible. Although it is possible to stream to a mobile device, recorded music is still the best bet in some situations, such as in the car.

Key term

Connective
A word or phrase that links clauses or sentences together.

Unit 11 Know how to use paragraphs to organise your writing

Activity 1 — Choosing connectives

Choose connectives from the word bank to complete this text.

Catch-up TV means watching shows that have already been broadcast by using internet sites such as BBC iPlayer. According to OFCOM nearly 25 million people now watch catch-up TV and the numbers are set to rise further.

1 _____ catch-up TV is popular is that people don't have to arrange their lives to fit in with TV programme schedules any more. 2 _____, if two programmes that they like are on at the same time, they don't have to miss one.

3 _____, there are drawbacks to watching online. If your broadband is on the slow side, you will have to sit waiting and your programme may even conk out in the middle. It always happens just at the exciting part!

4 _____ problem for catch-up TV watchers is spoilers. If your friends and colleagues have already watched the last episode of that crime thriller, they might let slip who did it and spoil your enjoyment.

5 _____, being able to watch TV programmes when you want and not when the broadcasters think best is just so convenient that the drawbacks seem quite small.

Connectives word bank

the main reason / most importantly / my first point is that / another / in addition

another reason / also / in addition / secondly / furthermore /

moreover / besides / lastly / finally / in conclusion / therefore / as / because / in order to / so that / as a result of / due to / a reason for this / therefore / nevertheless / on the other hand / however

Activity 2 — Using your own connectives

Write your own text and underline the connectives that link your paragraphs together. You could write about advantages and disadvantages of listening to music in different media – radio, streaming, CDs, downloads.

Feedback

I can:

→ use connecting words and phrases to link my paragraphs together.

125

UNIT 12 Know how to use verbs effectively

1 Using verbs so your meaning is clear

Learning objective

I *am learning how to:*
→ *understand subject/verb agreement*
→ *use tricky verbs when writing in Standard English.*

Key term

Subject/verb agreement
Verbs sometimes have to take a different form so that they agree with their subject.

In English, most verbs only make one change because of the rules of **subject/verb agreement:** they add -s if the subject is not I, you or a plural noun. For example:

I talk	We talk	
You talk	They talk	He/she/it/the parrot **talks**

Some very common verbs make different changes:

I am	We are	
You are	They are	He/she/it/the parrot **is** here

I was	We were	
You were	They were	He/she/it/the parrot **was** here

I have	We have	
You have	They have	He/she/it/the parrot **has** a nut

Mistakes can arise if you don't identify correctly whether the subject of the verb is singular or plural.

Other mistakes happen because Standard English sometimes differs from forms of the verb used in local speech.

Activity 1 — Adding -s

When the subject of a verb is he/she/it or a singular noun, the verb adds

126

Unit 12 Know how to use verbs effectively

1 Apply this rule in these sentences.

The children _____ in lessons. (speak/speaks)
The game _____ in ten minutes. (start/starts)
Glass bottles _____ easily. (break/breaks)

Activity 2 Using the correct form

Use the Standard English form of the verb *to be* in these sentences.

The radio programme (was/were) really funny.
I (be/am/is/are) a comedian.
We (was/were) running as fast as we could.
When the band played it (was/were) very loud.
I (be/am/is/are) going to the shops.
The swans (be/is/are) flying above the lake.

Activity 3 Identifying the correct form

Put in the correct form of the verb. Think carefully about whether the subject of the verb is singular or plural.

The team always (plays/play) fairly.
A pack of dogs (is/are) terrorising the village.
Bottles of medicine (is/are) kept in a locked cupboard.
Jayden, unlike all his friends, (like/likes) drama.
A plate of sausages (was/were) very tempting.
Tons of earth and rock regularly (fall/falls) down the cliff face.
No one except his enemies (want/wants) him to fail.
None of us (enjoys/enjoy) opera apart from my dad.

Feedback

I can:
→ use verbs accurately by making the verb in a sentence agree with the subject
→ use Standard English forms of the verb *to be*.

2 Using verb tenses

Learning objective

I am learning how verb tenses affect the meaning of what I write, including:

➡ *present, past, future*
➡ *using verb tenses consistently*
➡ *using verb tenses for effect.*

Key term

Verb tense
Verbs change their form to indicate the time at which an action takes place. These changes are called tenses.

Verbs tell us whether an event happens in the present, the past or the future.

Present	Past	Future
They talk	They talked	They will talk
They are talking	They were talking	
	They have talked	

> The present tense can also be used to describe things that are always true: 'Two and two make four.'

> Regular verbs show the past tense by adding -ed.

Activity 1   Using the correct tense

Put the verb into these sentences using the correct tense. Read the whole sentence and work out if the verb needs to be in the present, past or future tense. Then select the correct form of the verb.

- He _____ into the river right now. (jump)
- They _____ the work before they started writing. (discuss)
- I _____ in England for three years already and I plan to stay longer. (live)
- 'Mr Jones _____ you a test tomorrow,' said the teacher. (give)
- The team _____ every penalty last season. (miss)
- The hunter spotted the footprint and then _____ the animal to its den. (track)

128

Unit 12 Know how to use verbs effectively

| Activity 2 | Being consistent |

When you are writing you need to make sure that you use verb tenses consistently so the reader is not confused. If you are describing events that happened in the past you should keep to the past tense.

Correct the underlined verbs in this text to make it consistent.

> Yesterday morning Jo ran to the newsagent to get her magazine. She <u>walk</u> back though because she felt too hot. On the way she <u>spy</u> her friend Elaine waiting at the bus stop. She <u>talking</u> with a boy! Jo stopped and <u>look</u> carefully. She just <u>stare</u>. She thought she <u>recognise</u> him or did she?

• •

| Activity 3 | Changing tense to make an impact |

In a story it is possible to switch from the past to the present tense to make the action seem more dramatic. Look at this example:

> The soldiers walked in single file through the thick jungle. It was very hot and sticky and they were dog-tired. They wearily entered a small clearing and stopped for a breather.
>
> A strange silence sucked in all the usual jungle noises for a moment and then all hell broke loose. Bullets whip through the leaves and branches. A small explosion throws dirt and bits of tree through the air. Men dive for cover, and flatten themselves to the ground. The Lieutenant shouts an order but nobody hears it. Then the very ground itself heaves upwards with a deafening roar.

1 **Can you identify where the author changes to the present tense for dramatic effect?**

2 **Write your own action story paragraph where you use this technique.**

Feedback

I can:

→ see the difference between present, past and future verb tenses

→ use the past tense consistently in a story

→ use a change of tense deliberately to create an effect.

3 Using tricky verbs accurately

Learning objective

I am learning how to:
→ *use irregular verbs*
→ *use Standard English forms of the past tense*
→ *use modal verbs.*

Key terms

Irregular verbs
There are about 300 verbs in English that do not follow the regular pattern in their present and past tenses. Many of the 300 are commonly used words.

Modal verbs
These 'help' a main verb by expressing additional meaning.

Mistakes in writing can happen with verbs because the Standard English form of the past tense is irregular and may well be different from the form commonly used in speech. For example:

People may say: 'I've took the book back.'

You need to write: 'I have taken the book back.'

Activity 1 Getting tricky verbs right

Complete the verbs in these sentences in Standard English. If you are not sure, you can search on the internet under 'English irregular verbs'.

- I have _____ my pen. (break)
- He has _____ his tongue. (bite)
- You have _____ an excellent book. (choose)
- She has _____ a car like this before. (drive)
- We have _____ in this cafe many times. (eat)
- The walker had _____ off the cliff in foggy weather. (fall)
- The boy had _____ his pencil. (forget)
- All the students were _____ prizes. (give)
- The squirrel has _____ nuts all over the garden. (hide)
- People in flats can be _____ up by neighbours playing loud music. (wake)

Unit 12 Know how to use verbs effectively

Activity 2 — Researching tricky verbs

1 Find out how these verbs are formed in the past tense:

> begin, drink, ring, sing, sink, stink, swim

2 Write two short sentences for each past tense verb. For example:

> I began to run away.
> I have begun to learn German.

Handwritten note:
past simple
- when detailed time or place action took place are given
- action started & finished in past ie not happening now

pres. perfect
- action started in past & is still happening now or happens regularly
- when time of action not specified & not important

Activity 3 — Using modal verbs to express shades of meaning

The main modal verbs are:

| Can/could | May/might | Will/would | Shall/should |

likelihood or ability.

1 What is the difference in meaning between these pairs of sentences? Think carefully about the meaning that is added by the modal verb. *(handwritten: doubt & conditional on sth)*

> I can go to the cinema on Saturday.
> I could go to the cinema on Saturday.
> You may go home if it rains.
> You might go home if it rains.
>
> I will help you clear up.
> I would help you clear up.
> I shall always remember your birthday.
> I should always remember your birthday.

2 Write sentences of your own using these modal verbs and ask a partner to think about the meaning you have expressed.

Feedback

I can:

→ use the Standard English forms of some common irregular verbs in English

→ understand how modal verbs add meaning to the main verb in a sentence.

131

UNIT 13 Know how to spell words

1 Know how to spell words with quiet or hidden sounds

Learning objective

I am learning how to spell words with quiet or hidden sounds.

Key term

Unstressed
Part of a word that is hard to hear when it is spoken.

One way of remembering how to spell a word is to think about how it sounds, but this can lead to mistakes with some words. There is a group of words that have quiet or hidden sounds or letters because when we say them part of the word is **unstressed**. For example: int*e*rest – spoken as *intrest*.

[Hidden sound]

Activity 1 Recognise unstressed or hidden sounds in words

Write these words and highlight or underline the part with the unstressed or hidden sound:

- business
- factory
- history
- Wednesday
- deafening
- fattening
- library
- different
- general
- vegetable

Activity 2 Learn words with unstressed or hidden sounds

A good trick for learning words with unstressed or hidden sounds is called speak-spell.

To use speak-spell when you learn a word, say the word to yourself as it is spelled instead of the way you normally say it. Say *in-ter-rest* to remember the spelling of *interest*. Put plenty of stress on the sound that is normally unstressed and say the word in an exaggerated way if it helps.

Unit 13 **Know how to spell words**

1 Say these words in speak-spell either to yourself or to your partner and then write them without copying. Check if you have spelt them correctly. Try again if not!

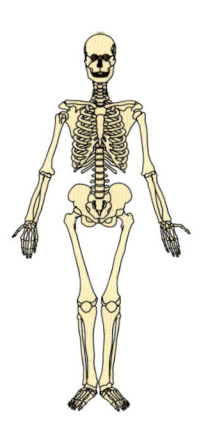

- boundary
- conference
- definite
- describe
- environment
- family
- geography
- marvellous
- offering
- medicine
- similar
- skeleton

| Activity 3 | Learn common words with quiet or hidden sounds |

Look at this list of common words that have unstressed or hidden sounds.

1 Highlight or underline the unstressed or hidden sounds.

2 Now ask your partner to test you on the words.

3 Use the speak-spell trick to learn the words you couldn't spell correctly.

4 Let your partner test you again.

If you are working on your own, look at each word in the list quickly once, cover and then try to write. Use speak-spell to learn any words that you couldn't spell correctly without copying them.

bound**a**ry	famili**a**r	lott**e**ry
bus**i**ness	fam**i**ly	marv**e**llous
categ**o**ry	fatt**e**ning	math**e**matics
conf**e**rence	Febru**a**ry	med**i**cine
deaf**e**ning	g**e**ography	mem**o**rable
def**i**nite	hist**o**ry	off**e**ring
d**e**scribe	int**e**rested	sim**i**lar
desp**e**rate	lib**r**ary	skel**e**ton
diff**e**rence	lit**e**racy	veg**e**table
fact**o**ry	lit**e**rature	wid**e**ning

Feedback

I can:

➔ recognise unstressed or hidden sounds in a word

➔ use the speak-spell strategy to learn words like this

➔ spell 30 common words with unstressed or hidden sounds.

133

2 Know how to spell plural nouns

Learning objective

I am learning how to spell the plural form of nouns.

Key term

Plural

'More than one'. Most nouns have a plural form, which changes their spelling.

Rules for spelling plural nouns

Most nouns add the letter s at the end for their plural form.

One duck. Two duck**s**. Twenty duck**s**.

Some words that end with a hissing or a buzzing sound add -es for their plural form.

One fox. Two fox**es**. One dish. Two dish**es**. One watch. Two watch**es**.

Words ending in a consonant followed by the letter -y change the y to an i and add -es for their plural form.

One fly. Two fli**es**. One puppy. Two pupp**ies**.

Most words ending in -f or -fe lose the f and add -ves for their plural form.

One wolf. Two wol**ves**. One knife. Two kni**ves**.

Activity 1 Identify plural nouns

Read the text and find all the plural nouns. Tip: words ending in -s are not always plurals – look for words telling you about **more than one**.

Wen was mad about lists. Some of the lists she had pinned to her noticeboard included:

- My shoes
- Things I do on Wednesdays
- Why babies are cute
- The wives of Henry the Eighth
- Excuses Mum gives for being late

If a friend asks about Wen's lists, she says, 'Writing a list makes me feel calm.'

Unit 13 Know how to spell words

Activity 2 — Recognise words that add -es for the plural

Put these words into two lists: a) Words that add -s to make a plural and b) Words that add -es to make a plural.

Remember that words ending with a hissing, buzzing or shushing sound add -es.

church	banana	kiss	prince	patch
bus	lunch	frog	box	dish

Activity 3 — Spell the plural form of words ending in -y

Remember the rule:

> Words ending in a consonant followed by the letter -y change the y to an i and add -es for their plural form.

Key term

Consonant
Any letter that is **not** a vowel (a, e, i, o, u).

Write the plural form of these words.

baby	boy	ice-lolly	party	curry
fly	monkey	city	key	jelly

Activity 4 — Spell the plural form of words ending in -f and -fe

Remember the rule:

> Most words ending in -f or -fe lose the f and add -ves for their plural form.

half	thief	knife
loaf	roof (Exception alert! Check the dictionary.)	wife
scarf		wolf
self		

Feedback

I can:
- → recognise plural nouns
- → remember the main spelling rules for plural nouns
- → learn plurals that do not follow the rules.

3 Know how to spell verb endings

Learning objective

I am learning how to spell words which add -ing and -ed at the end.

Key term

Past tense
The form of a verb that we use when we are talking about something that happened in the past.

The rules about adding -ing and -ed to the end of words are easy to learn.

Most English verbs add -ed to make the **past tense** and -ing for some other forms. For example, see the verb *to talk*:

I **talk**.

I **talk**ed.

I am **talk**ing.

I was **talk**ing.

Still **talk**ing, he left the room.

Learning the rules about adding -ed and -ing endings will help you avoid some common spelling mistakes.

Activity 1 — Spelling verb endings: Rule 1

Most verbs do not change their spelling when they add -ed and -ing.

Use this rule to complete these sentences using the correct form of the verb:

- walk

  Yesterday I _____ to school.

Unit 13 Know how to spell words

- speak

  I was _____ to my friend just last week.
- follow

  Because I patted it, the dog _____ me home.
- destroy

  In the last century an earthquake _____ the town.
- experiment

  Last lesson we were _____ with magnets and iron filings.

Activity 2 Spelling verb endings: Rule 2

Verbs ending in the letter e drop the e and then add -ed or -ing.

Use this rule to complete these sentences using the correct form of the verb.

- phone

  I _____ them before I went to their house.
- smile

  We were both _____.
- bake

  I am _____ a cake for a competition.
- like

  Most people _____ the show last night.
- share

  He was _____ the sweets with his friends.
- use

  She was _____ the computer to write an email.

3 Know how to spell verb endings

- hope

    They were _____ for good weather on the trip.

- practise

    The team _____ last Thursday.

- surprise

    I was _____ by a loud noise.

- receive

    He _____ the letter earlier this morning.

Activity 3   Spelling verb endings: Rule 3

> For verbs ending with a **short vowel sound** and a single consonant, double the consonant and add -ed or -ing.

Example: slip

I slipped on the ice.

The cars were slipping sideways on the icy road.

Use this rule to complete these sentences using the correct form of the verb.

- tip

    The truck was _____ soil into the hole.

- stop

    The signal was red so the train _____.

- tap

    A little bird was _____ on the window.

- hug

    _____ her teddy, the girl wandered off.

138

Unit 13 Know how to spell words

- let

  'I'm _____ you go on the trip,' said Mum.

- knit

  Nana _____ me a jumper in a strange colour.

- plan

  The prisoners were _____ their escape.

- begin

  The book was _____ to get exciting.

- clap

  The audience _____ until the band played more.

- hop

  The frog _____ off the rock into the pond.

Feedback

→ I know about verbs adding -ed and -ing

→ I know the three rules of spelling for adding -ed and -ing

→ I can apply the rules to spell verbs ending in -ed and -ing correctly.

4 Know how to spell common letter clusters

Learning objective

I am learning how to spell words with common letter clusters.

Key term

Letter cluster
A group of letters that often come together in words.

The English spelling system contains some groups of letters that often appear together. Remembering these can improve your spelling. What can be tricky, however, is that the letter clusters may make more than one sound.

Activity 1　Practise writing letter clusters

In joined-up handwriting, write out each of these letter clusters ten times:

- ight
- ough
- ice
- ear

Try to write each cluster in one flowing movement. This will help your hand to remember them!

Activity 2　Learn words with the -ight cluster

1 Look at this list of words containing -ight. Can you add any more?

bright	freight	might	sight
eight	height	night	tight
fight	light	right	weight

2 Write the words out in two groups with words that rhyme together in each group.

3 Ask a partner to test your spelling of these words.

Unit 13 Know how to spell words

Activity 3 — Learn words with the -ough cluster

1 Look at this list of words containing -ough.

| bough | cough | though | thought | tough |
| enough | thorough | through | plough | |

2 Write the words out in groups of words where -ough makes the same sound.

3 How many different sounds did you find for -ough?

4 Write a five-sentence paragraph using as many of the -ough words as possible. Use a dictionary if necessary.

Activity 4 — Learn words with the -ice cluster

1 Look at this list of words containing -ice. Can you add any more?

| Alice | apprentice | dice | notice | practice | rice |
| mice | twice | spice | nice | | |

2 Write the words out in two groups with words that rhyme together in each group.

3 Ask a partner to test your spelling of these words.

Activity 5 — Learn words with the -ear cluster

1 Look at this list of words containing -ear. Can you add any more?

| bear | dear | earth | fear | learn | wear |
| dreary | earn | gear | weary | hear | |

2 Write the words out in groups of words where -ear makes the same sound.

3 Ask a partner to test your spelling of these words.

Feedback

I know how to spell words with the letter cluster:
➔ -ight
➔ -ough
➔ -ice
➔ -ear.

5 Know how to spell homophones

Learning objective

I am learning how to:

➜ *spell common homophones*

➜ *invent mnemonics to help me remember spellings.*

Key terms

Homophones
Words with the same sound but with different spellings and meanings.

Mnemonic
A memory trick to help you remember something.

There are two kinds of homophones:

- Words that sound the same, are spelled the same, but have different meanings, such as *rose*.
  The sun rose at eight o'clock. The rose is a beautiful flower.
- Words that sound the same but are spelled differently and have a different meaning, such as *male* and *mail*.
  They needed a male actor for the part. The postman brought some mail.

This section focuses on the second type of homophone, and shows that mnemonics can be a good way of remembering how to spell homophones, which are very easy to mix up.

Activity 1   Commonly used homophones

These are the most commonly used homophones:

there:	a place (*You'll find it over there.*)
	a pronoun (*There are two ways to do it.*)
their:	means belonging to them (*It is their present so give it to them.*)
they're:	a shortened form of they are (*They're going shopping.*)

142

Unit 13 Know how to spell words

to: a handy little word used in a number of ways – this is the most common way of spelling this sound (*I am going to school. I want to learn.*)

too: as well, in addition (*My brother wanted some cake too.*)

two: the number 2 (*Use two hands to steer the car.*)

its: belonging to it (*The monster appeared. It was so close, I could see its tiny eyes.*)

it's: shortened form of it is (*It's mine = It is mine*)

For each of these three, we could imagine a picture with a caption using the different spellings. For example:

They're sitting **there** eating **their** bananas.

Think of your own pictures and captions for the three sets of homophones. The funnier or more unusual the picture, the more likely you are to remember it.

Activity 2 — Commonly used homophones

Here is a list of 20 homophones that commonly cause spelling mistakes.

aloud	bean	break	flour	grate
allowed	been	brake	flower	great
here	herd	hole	know	meet
hear	heard	whole	no	meat
new	right	peace	plane	see
knew	write	piece	plain	sea
stair	steel	stationary	through	week
stare	steal	stationery	threw	weak

143

5 Know how to spell homophones

1 Use a dictionary to check the meaning of any words you are unsure of.

2 These are some mnemonics that people use to remember the difference between the pairs:

- The words 'hear' and 'heard' are about listening and contain the word 'ear'.
- The word 'meat' contains the word 'eat'.
- 'Stationery' is spelled with an e and includes **e**nvelopes.
  Invent your own mnemonics to help you remember the difference between the pairs. Your mnemonic could be a picture with a silly caption or anything about the words that helps you remember which word is which.

Activity 3 Use the correct homophone

Fill the gaps in these sentences with the correct homophones.

- _____ standing over _____ with _____ friends. (there, their, they're)
- I find it _____ hard _____ do _____ things at once. (to, too, two)
- _____ not what you do _____ the way that you do it. (its, it's)
- I'd like a _____ of cake. (peace, piece)
- The _____ stampeded across the field. (herd, heard)
- I'll _____ you at the bus-stop. (meat, meet)
- Can you eat a _____ pizza? (hole, whole)
- First _____ the cheese into a bowl. (great, grate)
- He _____ the ball _____ the window. (through, threw)
- Only children under ten were _____ to travel free. (aloud, allowed)

Unit 13 Know how to spell words

Activity 4 — Find the homophones

Find the homophones for these words and write short sentences to show what they mean.

bear	heel
berry	root
sell	sent
hair	stare
hall	waste

Handwritten notes:
bare, bury, cell, hare, haul
heal, route, scent, stair, waist

Activity 5 — Identify noun and verb homophones

Some words that sound the same (or nearly the same) are spelled differently depending on whether they are being used as a noun or a verb. Do some detective work with a dictionary to find out which of these pairs is the verb and which is the noun.

- ✓ practise   n practice
- n effect   ✓ affect
- n licence   ✓ license *(in US, it's both noun & verb)*
- n advice   ✓ advise
- n prophecy   ✓ prophesy

> **Feedback**
>
> I know:
> - about homophones
> - how to invent mnemonics that help me stop mixing up homophones
> - how to spell the most common homophones.

145

6 Know how to add suffixes

Learning objective

I am learning how to spell words that add suffixes.

Key term

Suffix

Letters added to the end of a word to change its grammatical function or meaning.
Sometimes a suffix makes the base word into a verb, and sometimes into an adjective, noun or adverb. Sometimes the suffix changes the tense of a verb.

Here is an example of a base word and a suffix.

Base word	Suffix	New word
loud	-ly	loudly

Words add suffixes for different reasons. In this example the suffix changes an adjective into an adverb.

Look at these examples with the suffixes in red.

hard	hard**er**	hard**est**
quick	quick**ly**	
hope	hope**ful**	
home		home**less**

These examples demonstrate this rule:

> For most words the spelling of the base word does not change when you add these suffixes.

But

> Words ending in a y change the y to i when they add these suffixes.

For example:

Base word	Suffix	New word
beauty	ful	beautiful

146

Unit 13 Know how to spell words

Activity 1	Add suffixes

Make as many words as you can by adding these suffixes to the base words. Remember to apply the spelling rule.

-ly
-ful
-less

care   hungry   colour
mercy   fear   speedy
friend   success   happy
pain   slow
pity   harm

By adding suffixes you should be able to make 21 new words.

Activity 2	Use the spelling rule for suffixes

Look at this rhyme.

> Down behind the shed
> I saw a **heavy** bed.
> It was **heavier** than mine
> The **heaviest** I've seen.

1 Now complete the rest of the verses using the suffixes -er and -est.

> Down behind the shed
> I saw a **pretty** head.
> It was _____ than mine
> The _____ I've seen.

> Down behind the hedge
> I saw a **speedy** sledge.
> It was _____ than mine
> The _____ I've seen.

147

6 Know how to spell homophones

Down behind the hedge
I saw a **tiny** wedge.
It was _____ than mine
The _____ I've seen.

Down behind the bin
I saw a **wide** grin.
It was _____ than mine
The _____ I've seen.

Down behind the bin
I saw a **sharp** pin.
It was _____ than mine
The _____ I've seen.

Down behind the shed
I saw a **strong** thread.
It was _____ than mine
The _____ I've seen.

Down behind the bin
I saw a **hairy** chin.
It was _____ than mine
The _____ I've seen.

Down behind the bin
I saw a **wide** grin.
It was _____ than mine
The _____ I've seen.

Down behind the bin
I saw a **shiny** tin.
It was _____ than mine
The _____ I've seen.

Down behind the bin
I saw a **skinny** twin.
She was _____ than mine
The _____ I've seen.

Unit 13 Know how to spell words

2 Make up some verses of your own using the same pattern. What did you find behind the wall? Was it a ball, a shawl or a hall?

Activity 3   Learn problem words

There are some words that get tricky when they add suffixes.

Here are two very tricky ones that you will have to learn.

skill – skilful

whole – wholly

Only very skilful spellers get these words right!

These words are also tricky but can you work out the rule that they follow?

probable – probably

enjoyable – enjoyably

miserable – miserably

Feedback

I know:

→ about suffixes

→ the rule that tells me how to spell words when they add the suffixes -ful, -ess, -ly, -er, -est

→ how to spell some tricky words with suffixes.

UNIT 14 Know how to choose language to affect your reader

1 Know how to choose words for impact

Learning objective

I am learning how to choose words that will make an impact on my reader.

Key terms

Impact
The effect you want to have on your reader.
Synonyms
Words with similar meanings.

Good writers choose their words carefully. They try to use words that are interesting and effective. They also try not to use the same word too often.

Activity 1 Notice words that could be improved

1 Choose three words in this text that you could change to make it more interesting and descriptive.

> The snow came down. The large flakes moved in the wind. 'Let's go out and do snowballs,' said Jo. She stood up and went to the door.

2 Now see if you can think of three more descriptive words to use. You can use a thesaurus to help you.

Activity 2 Choose words for interest

1 Look at this piece of writing. Replace each of the highlighted words with a word from the brackets.

> Suddenly I could hear the **sound** (scream, howl, moan, groan) of a siren.
> A police car **came** (swerved, raced, appeared, flew) into view.

150

Unit 14 Know how to choose language to affect your reader

'Where's that going?' **said** (shouted, asked, shrieked, whined) my brother.

'To the scrap yard,' I **said** (replied, yelled, whispered, murmured).

At once we **went** (charged, scampered, ran, sprinted) towards it.

2 Now explain why you chose the words you did.

Activity 3 — Choose words to affect your reader's point of view

1 Read this description of a sandwich. Choose the words from the brackets that would most make someone want to eat it.

Our (outstanding, regular, least popular) club sandwich (contains, is filled to bursting with, has a bit of) ham from a local (farm, factory, warehouse, pig-sty), (shiny, dry, flavoursome, sweaty) slices of cheese with (fruity, smelly, mouth-watering, sticky) chutney. We only use our own famous bread which is (re-heated, freshly baked, stale, crumbly) every day.

2 Now select the words that would most make someone *not* want to eat it.

Activity 4 — Choose your own words

Choose your own words to fill the gaps in this advertisement for a new car. You want to make the car attractive to motorists who like comfort, style and speed.

You will love our new sport coupé with its _____ body shape that comes in a range of _____, _____ colours.

Sit inside and it's _____. Drive it in town and it's _____. On the open road it's _____.

You will look so _____ in the new sport coupé.

Feedback

I can choose words to make:

→ writing more interesting to the reader

→ a reader react in a certain way

151

2 Know how to choose words to match a topic

Learning objective

I am learning to use precise words in instructions.

It is important to use precise vocabulary when writing instructions or information texts. It makes things clear to the reader. Different kinds of writing, such as recipes or science experiments, have their own precise words.

Activity 1 Identify precise words

Recipes need to use precise words to make sure the food turns out as it should.

1 Pick out five examples of precise words from this recipe.

Scones

Ingredients

- 180g self-raising flour
- Half a tablespoon caster sugar
- 40g butter
- 125ml milk

Method

- Preheat oven to 220°C / Gas 7. Dust a baking tray with self-raising flour.
- Sieve flour into a bowl. Add caster sugar. Using your fingertips, rub butter into the mixture until it looks like fine breadcrumbs.
- Add milk. Mix until dough begins to come together. Turn out onto a lightly floured surface and knead gently until dough comes together.
- Flatten dough with palm of your hand until about 2cm thick. Use a 5cm round cutter or a drinking glass to cut out your scones. Place onto a baking tray. Brush with leftover milk.
- Bake in preheated oven for 14–16 minutes or until golden.

Unit 14 Know how to choose language to affect your reader

2 Are the precise words you have chosen nouns or verbs or adjectives?

3 Why do verbs need to be precise in a recipe?

Activity 2 — Choose precise words

1 Improve this set of instructions by replacing the highlighted words with words that are more precise and are a better match for a science experiment. Choose from these words and phrases:

> beaker   absorb   repeat   the volume extracted
> stopwatch   measuring cylinder   insert
> note the result in a data table

Experiment

Do different types of paper towel **suck up** different amounts of water?

You need:

- Several types of paper towel
- A **clock**
- A **container**
- A **measuring thing**
- A funnel

Method

a) Fill the **container** up with exactly 200ml of water.

b) Take a sheet of the first type of towel.

c) Fold and **stick** into the water. As you dip the towel into the water, start your **clock**.

d) After 20 seconds, remove the towel from the **container** and squeeze as much water as you can out of the towel into the **measuring thing** using the funnel. Make a note of **what came out**.

e) **Do it again** four times for each type and **write it down**.

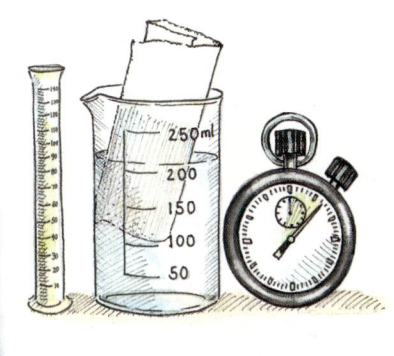

Feedback

→ I can identify and choose precise words that match a topic.

153

3 Know how to use writers' techniques

Learning objective

I am learning to use some writers' techniques.

Writers use a wide range of techniques to add interest and quality to their writing and to enhance meaning. In this section you will learn about three easy-to-use techniques.

- **Specific words**

  Instead of writing 'tree', you can write 'beech', 'oak' or 'elm'.

- **Repetition**

  Repeat a word or phrase to add emphasis.

- **Word music**

  Sometimes writers want to do more than just describe something; they want what they write to sound good to your ears.

Activity 1 | Use specific words

> The lad departed, and Durbeyfield lay waiting on the grass and daisies in the evening sun.

In his novel *Tess of the d'Urbervilles,* Thomas Hardy didn't write 'Durbeyfield lay waiting on the **ground**', he used more specific words.

1 **Improve these sentences by changing the highlighted words to something more specific.**

- A **bird** perched on the fence.
- James sat at the bar and carefully moved his **drink** a little closer to him.

154

Unit 14 Know how to choose language to affect your reader

- As he walked up the path, he was met by a barking **dog**.
- Rokia **went** from one side of the **room** to another again and again.
- As Hammond turned the corner, the **building** reared up in front of him.

2 Now write three sentences of your own and underline the words or phrases where you have used specific words.

Activity 2 | Repeat words for effect

1 a) Read this extract from the start of the novel *Bleak House* by Charles Dickens.

> Fog everywhere. Fog up the river, where it flows among green **aits** and meadows; fog down the river, where it rolls defiled among the tiers of shipping and the waterside pollutions of a great (and dirty) city. Fog on the Essex marshes, fog on the Kentish **heights**. Fog creeping into the **cabooses** of **collier-brigs**; fog lying out on the yards, and hovering in the rigging of great ships; fog drooping on the **gunwales** of barges and small boats. Fog in the eyes and throats of ancient Greenwich pensioners, wheezing by the firesides of their wards; fog in the stem and bowl of the afternoon pipe of the wrathful **skipper**, down in his close cabin; fog cruelly pinching the toes and fingers of his shivering little **'prentice boy** on deck.

Expand your vocabulary

aits – small islands
heights – high ground
cabooses – kitchens
collier-brigs – two-masted sailing ships carrying coal
gunwales – the upper edge of the ship's side
skipper – captain
'prentice boy – young apprentice

b) In this extract the word 'fog' is repeated eleven times. What effect does this have on you as you read?

What do you know about … *Bleak House*?

Bleak House is a novel by Charles Dickens published in 20 instalments in 1852. The story aims to expose the weakness of the justice system in England. In this extract the fog represents the confusion in the courts.

3 Know how to use writers' techniques

2 a) Read this poem by James Reeves.

b) Why do you think the poet repeats the word 'slowly' like this? What effect is he trying to achieve?

Slowly

Slowly the tide creeps up the sand,

Slowly the shadows cross the land.

Slowly the cart horse pulls his mile,

Slowly the old man mounts the stile.

Slowly the hands move round the clock,

Slowly the dew dries on the dock.

Slow is the snail – but slowest of all

The green moss spreads on the old brick wall.

3 Write a piece of your own in which you use the technique of repetition. It could be a poem like 'Slowly' ('Quickly' is a possible topic), or it could be a descriptive paragraph like the one from *Bleak House* (a snow scene perhaps).

> **Key term**
>
> **Alliteration**
> Putting words together that have the same sound at the start.

Activity 3 — Make it sound good

In his poem 'Wind', Ted Hughes wrote:

> A black-back gull bent like an iron bar slowly.

Notice how using a number of words beginning with b close together helps to make this line sound good. This technique is called alliteration.

Unit 14 Know how to choose language to affect your reader

Here is another example. This is taken from 'The Rime of the Ancient Mariner' by Samuel Taylor Coleridge.

> The fair breeze blew, the white foam flew,
> The furrow followed free;
> We were the first that ever burst
> Into that silent sea.

1 **Identify where alliteration is used in this verse. Annotate a printed copy or use sticky notes.**

2 **Write a short descriptive paragraph about this photograph in which you use some alliteration to help your writing sound special.**

Feedback

I can:

→ choose specific words in my writing
→ use the technique of repetition to create an effect
→ use alliteration to make my writing sound good.

157

4 Know how to use words and phrases imaginatively

Learning objective

I am learning to use language in an imaginative way.

All good writers try to work their reader's imagination and make them 'see' what they are writing about in a new way. Using similes and metaphors is a way to do this.

In his poem about a windy day Andrew Young uses a simile and a metaphor to describe a field with cattle in it:

> The fields that are a flowing sea
> And make the cattle look like ships

In this **simile** using the word 'like', the cattle are compared to ships sailing through the field of grass.

Key terms

Simile
Describing something by comparing it to something else using the words 'like' or 'as'.

Metaphor
A word picture that brings something to life by describing it as if it *is* something else.

The wind is blowing the grass so it looks like waves. This is a **metaphor** because it states that the fields are the sea.

Activity 1 — Use similes

Use your imagination to complete these descriptive similes.
- The snow covered the roof like …
- The cat crept towards the mouse as quietly as …
- Clouds, like …, gathered in the sky.
- The fly buzzed against the window with a sound like …
- Mrs Jones was not pleased. Her face was like …

Activity 2 — Use metaphors

1 Answer these questions about yourself.
- If you were an animal, what would you be?
- If you were a book, what would you be?

Unit 14 Know how to choose language to affect your reader

- If you were a kind of food, what would you be?
- If you were a building, what kind of building would you be?
- If you were a kind of weather, what would you be?

One boy wrote a description of himself, turning his answers into metaphors.

> I am the cat that walks on its own. I am the textbook left on the bus. I am a curry – a little bit spicy and not to everybody's taste. Walk past me and you walk past a little corner shop that never has what you want. Sunshine and showers – that's me.

2 Use your own answers to write a description of yourself using metaphors in the same sort of way.

Activity 3 Use your own similes and metaphors

Write a description based on this picture of a tornado. Try to use at least one metaphor and one simile in what you write.

Feedback

→ I can describe things imaginatively using similes and metaphors.

159

5 Know how to use words with clarity and precision

Learning objective

I am learning how to choose words that carry the exact meaning I need to communicate.

Key term

Synonyms
Words with the same or very similar meanings.

English is a rich language with a very large number of words. Many words have synonyms – other words that have a similar but slightly different meaning. Good writers choose from synonyms carefully to ensure that they express themselves clearly and precisely. You can use a thesaurus, a dictionary of synonyms or the synonym tool in your word processing software program to find synonyms.

Activity 1 Investigate synonyms

Look at this sentence.

> Lola saw her friend and walked towards her.

The word 'walk' tells us what Lola did when she saw her friend. Using some synonyms of walk could make the meaning more precise.

Match the comments to the sentences.

1	Lola saw her friend and strode towards her.	a)	Lola wants to surprise her friend.
2	Lola saw her friend and tiptoed towards her.	b)	Lola wants to appear very confident.
3	Lola saw her friend and paced towards her.	c)	Lola has something urgent to say to her friend.
4	Lola saw her friend and sauntered towards her.	d)	Lola is not that keen to meet her friend now.
5	Lola saw her friend and skipped towards her.	e)	Lola is really happy to see her friend.

Unit 14 Know how to choose language to affect your reader

Activity 2 Choose synonyms

In these sentences choose the synonym that best matches the intended meaning.

- 'No, I can't,' said John in reply. (muttered, bellowed, exclaimed)
  John is not happy but is not confident about refusing.
- His neighbour threw the ball back over the fence. (tossed, hurled, lobbed)
  The neighbour is fed up with the ball coming into his garden.
- The glass was filled with cold water. (beaker, tumbler, goblet)
  The sentence comes from a science report.
- The smell of the dustbin reached his nose. (fragrance, whiff, stench)
  It is hot weather and the bin hasn't been emptied for two months.
- The curry was heating her mouth. (warming, burning, scorching)
  It was the spiciest curry on the menu.
- It was only eleven o'clock but they already felt hungry. (ravenous, starving, peckish)
  They weren't desperate to eat.
- The bee sting was painful. (agonising, sore, uncomfortable)
  It did not hurt very much.
- The comedian's jokes were funny. (side-splitting, hilarious, amusing)
  People weren't laughing out loud.

Activity 3 Choose words well in a description

Describe the flowers in this picture to the right as clearly and precisely as you can. Think carefully about the colour and shape of the flowers and leaves. Use a dictionary of synonyms, a thesaurus or your computer to add precision and clarity to your text.

Feedback

→ I can choose between synonyms to express meaning clearly and precisely.

161

6 Know how to use words to affect the reader's feelings

Learning objective

I am learning how to use emotive language.

Key term

Emotive language
Words chosen to have maximum impact on the reader's feelings.

Some words can arouse strong feelings. Writers choose to use these words when they want to influence their readers. Advertisers may want readers to feel positive about their product. Newspaper reporters may want us to feel angry about something or sympathetic to victims.

Look at these two versions of a news item.

Graffiti on New Statue

The new statue in Town Square has been defaced with graffiti. The damage will cost £5000 to put right.

Vandal **Ruins** Statue

The **pure white** marble of the **brand new** statue in Town Square is now covered with **a filthy, black scrawl**. Council tax payers will have to find £5000 **out of their own pockets** to put this **disgraceful mess** right.

The words highlighted in the second version are designed to have more impact on the reader's feelings.

Activity 1 — Recognise emotive language

Identify the words in this text that are meant to have an impact on your feelings.

Unit 14 Know how to choose language to affect your reader

Mrs Smith lay helpless on the hard floor, cold, thirsty and scared for three long hours while heartless care workers chatted and watched TV in a room not 20 metres away. The frail old lady's cries for help were repeatedly ignored as the unfeeling assistants scoffed an expensive box of chocolates they had mercilessly prised from her grip earlier.

Activity 2 Use emotive language

1 Add words and phrases to this newspaper article to strengthen the effect on the reader's feelings. Your aim for this article is to make the reader experience the horror and feel sorry for the victims.

Part of the main stand at United's ground fell down this afternoon. Many spectators were injured. The emergency services worked to free those who were trapped. Large numbers of fans with a range of injuries were taken to hospital by ambulance

Activity 3 Use emotive language to persuade

Write a short text with the aim of persuading young people to do more to protect endangered wildlife. Use emotive language to make them feel sorry for the animals that are dying out and angry at the people who are most responsible for this.

Feedback
→ I can choose words to influence the feelings of my reader.

UNIT 15 Know how to improve and shape your writing

1 Know how to collect ideas and plan

Learning objective — *I am learning how to plan a piece of writing.*

When you have a piece of writing to complete, there is usually some discussion about the topic that helps you think of what to write and how to write it. Sometimes though, for example in a test, you have to plan by yourself. Suppose you were asked to write descriptively about 'A visit to the fair' to share your experience with readers of your own age. You could write an account of a visit you have made or could imagine having made. You know, or can imagine, what happened but you will still need to:

- collect/remember ideas
- organise those ideas
- make a paragraph plan.

Activity 1 Collect ideas

A good way to collect ideas is to ask some key questions.

1 Complete this diagram to the left with your answers about 'A visit to the fair'.

(Diagram: *A visit to the fair* — Who? Where? When? What happened?)

Activity 2 Organise your ideas

Start to organise the information in your answers using bullet point lists under headings like this:

Unit 15 Know how to improve and shape your writing

> Setting the scene for the visit (who? where? when?)
>
> What happened (First, next ... In the end)

Activity 3 — Make a paragraph plan

It is important to think about paragraphs before you start writing and to have a good idea of how you will split your writing into sections. The way you have organised your ideas is a good starting point. A paragraph plan is a series of headings. Each heading sums up what is in the paragraph like this:

Paragraph	
1	Setting the scene for the visit
2	Arriving at the fairground – lights, noise, smells
3	Going on a good ride
4	Going on a disappointing ride
5	Trying to win a prize
6	Getting some food
7	Getting tired, running out of money and going home

Create a paragraph plan for your own piece of writing about a visit to the fair based on the ideas you collected and organised.

If you prefer, you can plan writing about a visit to another attraction.

Activity 4 — Move from planning to writing

Use your paragraph plan to complete a piece of writing. Remember that you can change your plan as you write if you need to. Write quickly to produce a first draft. The next unit will help you to improve your writing to produce a final draft.

Feedback

I can:

→ use questions to collect ideas

→ organise my ideas and make them into a paragraph plan before I start writing.

2 Understand the process of writing

Learning objective

I am learning how to improve the quality of the writing I do by:
➜ *writing a first draft*
➜ *reviewing my draft*
➜ *making improvements to my writing.*

Robert Burns, the eighteenth-century Scottish poet, might have jotted down in his notebook:

> My girl is like a red rose
> That's just come out in June
> My girl is like a song
> That's played in tune.

What we know is the first verse of his famous poem:

> O my Luve's like a red, red rose,
> That's newly sprung in June:
> O my Luve's like the melodie,
> That's sweetly play'd in tune.

Well, in those days spelling was still a bit flexible, but even the greatest writers have to work to craft their thoughts into good writing. Nobody gets it right first time.

This process is called drafting.

Key term

Drafting
A process of improving what you have first written until you are happy with the quality.

Activity 1 Learn how drafting works

The process of drafting works like this.

166

Unit 15 Know how to improve and shape your writing

First draft/Rough draft

Write quickly to get your ideas down. Don't forget to use punctuation and to try to spell words correctly even at this stage.

Review your first draft

Read through what you have written. If you can, it is a good idea to ask someone to look at it with you. Ask yourself these questions:

- Have I missed anything out?
- Does it all make sense?
- Is there anything I could cut out?
- Can I change some words to make it clearer for the reader, more interesting, more descriptive or more exciting?

Mark up your first draft

Use a pencil to make the changes on your first draft. Use crossing out, arrows and any other ways of showing what you want to change. Don't worry if it looks messy.

Final draft

Make your improvements. When writing your final draft remember to:

- check any spellings you are unsure of
- make an effort with presentation whether you are hand writing or using a keyboard.

Use this process to improve the piece of writing ('A visit to the fair') you did in the last section or another piece of writing you did recently.

Activity 2 — Draft a description

Look hard at this painting of sunflowers by Vincent van Gogh. Quickly write a first draft – one or two paragraphs – describing what you can see. Imagine that your piece of writing will be displayed next to the painting to add interest. Use the drafting process to produce a final piece of writing. Find another picture to use if you prefer.

Feedback

→ I can use the process of drafting to improve my writing.

3 Know how to edit your writing

Learning objective

I am learning how to make decisions about writing.

Look back to pages 164–165 where the process of drafting writing is set out. This section looks more closely at the process of reviewing a first draft: how to make the right decisions about what to change in the first draft.

Drafting is not just about correcting mistakes, it is about evaluating what you have written and thinking about how to improve it.

Remember: you want to impress your reader.

Activity 1	Identify four types of editing

When you are editing or revising a piece of writing you can decide on four types of action.

- **Add words**
- **Remove words**
- **Move words around**
- **Change words**

When you edit a first draft, you may well do all of these things.

Look at these examples.

Unit 15 Know how to improve and shape your writing

First draft	Edited draft
Adding words It was morning. Light flooded through the curtains into my eyes.	It was early morning. Dazzling light flooded through the thin curtains into my sleepy eyes.
Removing words Please take off your shoes before entering the room.	Take off shoes before entering.
Moving words around Black and vicious, the crows descended on the wounded rabbit.	The crows, black and vicious, descended on the wounded rabbit.
Changing words This was the bag I wanted. It was so cool.	This was the bag of my dreams. It was so stylish.

Look carefully at the editing changes that have been made in the examples. Why were they made? Has the writer succeeded in improving the writing?

Activity 2 Make it more descriptive

Look at this paragraph from a first draft. Make it more descriptive by adding some words.

> It was a road like any other. There were some shops and some houses. Along one side were some telegraph poles with wires between them. The road surface was poor with many potholes which had filled up with water to make puddles. A little way along was a car with no wheels. Beyond that a dustbin lay on its side with the lid some distance away.

Activity 3 Edit down

Some kinds of writing, such as instructions, need to be **concise**.

Edit this text by removing words to make it a more concise set of instructions. Try to reduce the length by half.

Key term

Concise
Writing that is concise says what it needs to say clearly but in few words.

169

3 Know how to edit your writing

Soft Boiled Eggs

It is likely that we all have our own idea about cooking boiled eggs. I think this is a good, reliable method that should suit everyone.

You need to find a small saucepan and put into it enough boiling water to cover the eggs by about 1cm. Next, quickly but gently lower the eggs into the water, one at a time, using a spoon. Use a timer and give the eggs one minute – no more, no less – in the boiling water.

Now take the pan off the stove, put a lid on it and set the timer again. How long you leave the eggs in the hot water will decide how soft they are. If you want an egg that has a liquid yolk and a white that is just about set, give the timer 6 minutes. If you want an egg with a firmer yolk and a white that is set hard, give the timer 7 minutes.

Activity 4 | Move words around

Try moving words around in these sentences to see if you can improve them.

'If you must, go to the party,' shouted Mum.

The red and gold, thick, curtains moved mysteriously.

Jane would take the bus into town to meet her friends tomorrow.

The room was wrecked: broken glass, splintered wood and burnt fabric.

Unit 15 Know how to improve and shape your writing

| Activity 5 | Change words |

Find more descriptive, interesting or effective words than the ones that are highlighted.

> 'What are you doing, Dad?' **said** John at the top of his voice.
>
> Out in the thunderstorm, they arrived home **wet**.
>
> Abbi was looking forward to English because they were reading a **good book**.
>
> You will need two **bits** of paper and a **little bit** of string.
>
> Tomorrow was the wedding. Ali needed some **nice** shoes, a **nice** dress and a **nice** hat. There was nothing like that in her wardrobe.

| Activity 6 | Edit your own work |

Take a piece of first draft writing of your own and show how you could edit it. Mark up your writing using the colours on the four types of editing shown on page 168.

Feedback

I can use the four types of editing to improve my work.

171

4 Know how to add the finishing touches

Learning objective

I am learning how to prepare a final draft by proofreading and making final corrections so that it is accurate and clear.

Writers want to respect their readers and to gain their respect in return. This means that the final version of your writing that you present to your reader should be:

- free from spelling mistakes
- punctuated so that the sentences are clear
- presented in a form that is clear and easy to read.

Activity 1   Make a proofreading checklist

Key term

Proofreading
A process of reading carefully to identify mistakes and put them right.

Everybody makes mistakes. You can even find mistakes in published books. Nevertheless, it is important to try to reduce the number of mistakes to a minimum. This will make a good impression on your reader and will mean more marks in an examination.

Spotting mistakes just by reading quickly through your writing is quite hard. Most people find that they are more likely to spot mistakes in their own work if they:

- leave a gap of time between finishing the writing and proofreading it
- print out the writing rather than check it on screen
- switch off all distractions, such as the TV, while proofreading.

People often repeat the same kind of mistakes in their writing again and again.

You can make a checklist of your own most common mistakes by looking back over written work that has been marked.

Unit 15 Know how to improve and shape your writing

Here is an example of such a list. It is important to make your own personal list – particularly if English is not your first language.

> My mistakes
> Confusing there and their
> Missing -s off the end of words
> Forgetting capital letters for proper nouns
> Using a comma when I should use a connective
> Forgetting apostrophes

Look back through your recent work (not just in English). See if there are mistakes that you have made a few times. Make your own personal proofreading checklist.

Activity 2 Practise proofreading

Identify and correct the mistakes in this writing. Use the checklist in Activity 1 to help you.

> On saturday I went round to my friends house. The idea was that I would help him mend a puncture on his bike, then go out for a ride. When I got their though, sam had already fixed his tyre, we could set off strait away.
>
> We decided to do a ride of about 30 miles, we were feeling fit. Their was no wind and it wasn't to hot, so we were really enjoying it. Unfortunately, after about ten miles Sams tyre was going flat again. We stopped and had a look, he couldn't have mended it properly. We tryed pumping it up but it wouldn't hold any air.
>
> I rode my bike back. Sam phoned his dad who came and fetched him in the car. Back at Sams, we mended the puncture together after all.

Feedback

I can:

→ identify mistakes I commonly make

→ use a checklist to proofread a text.

173

UNIT 16 Know how to focus your writing on audience and purpose

1 Understand the purposes for writing and different kinds of reader

Learning objective

I am learning to recognise how writing varies according to:
→ *different purposes*
→ *the target readership.*

Writing is used for a vast range of purposes from love letters to advertisements to parking tickets, not to mention plays, poems and novels.

How you write something will be strongly influenced by your purpose for writing it and who you expect to read it.

Activity 1 Identify different purposes

1 Match these beginnings to the most likely purpose of the text.

1	One upon a time in the forests of the West lived a large dragon.	a)	Comment on something
2	There are five steps to making a paper plane.	b)	Persuade
3	Last Tuesday turned out to be a very special day for me.	c)	Give factual information
4	Dragonflies are among the fastest flying insects in the world.	d)	Tell a story
5	From the very first paragraph the story grips you.	e)	Give instructions
6	The old woman's face was covered with deep wrinkles.	f)	Recount something that happened in real life
7	The car engine works like this.	g)	Discuss something
8	Singh's is the best ice cream. Here are five reasons why you should buy.	h)	Describe something
9	Is it ever right to go to war? There are two sides to this question.	i)	Explain something

Unit 16 Know how to focus your writing on audience and purpose

Activity 2 — Identify different readers

1 To the right are two images advertising gum. One is targeting an adult audience, the other targets children. Which is which?

2 Write your own short advertising texts for:

a) mint sweets with a target audience of i) adults, ii) children

b) a car with a target audience of i) wealthy business people, ii) young single women on small budget

c) a holiday resort with a target audience of i) young people who like to have a wild time, ii) older people who like peace and quiet.

Key term

Audience
In the context of writing this is the set of readers that the writer expects will read the text.

Activity 3 — Write for different purposes

Write three paragraphs about a product for sale. It could be a bike, a phone or anything you like. Each paragraph will be a separate piece of writing with a different purpose.

Paragraph 1

A description of the product with the purpose of giving factual information

Paragraph 2

A paragraph with the purpose of persuading someone to buy the product

Paragraph 3

A review of the product written by someone who has purchased one with the purpose of sharing comments on the item with people who might be thinking of buying

You could make it interesting by choosing to write about a very poor product which is made to sound very good in the persuasive writing.

Feedback

I can:

→ recognise different purposes for writing

→ see how to target different readers.

2 Know how to write stories

Learning objective

I am learning how to write a story.

A story is a sequence of events that happen over time. A good story, however, has to be more than just that.

This table shows the outline of a story using a simple three-part structure.

Basic story structure – 'The Liar'	
There were two friends who lived next door to each other. They did everything together.	Part 1 **Orientation** or setting the scene
Another boy/girl moves in across the street who tells lies that cause the friends to fight.	Part 2 **Complication** – a problem or a conflict
The liar is found out and the two friends make up.	Part 3 **Resolution** – the ending, which reveals how the problem or conflict is solved

To make it a good story it also needs some or all of these key features:

- **Description** – we need to be able to 'see' the story in our minds when we read it.
- **Characters** – we need to care about people in the story.
- A **narrative hook** – we need the reader to want to know what will happen. The narrative hook in 'The Liar' is that the reader knows the two friends have been tricked and wants them to find this out.

Key term

Narrative hook
Something that happens near the start of the story that makes the reader want to read on and find out more.

Activity 1 **Set the scene**

Make notes for the start of your version of 'The Liar' story. Make your notes under these headings:

- The two friends

176

Unit 16 Know how to focus your writing on audience and purpose

- The road where they live
- The new boy/girl who moves in

Remember that you will need some descriptive details about the place and you need to create characters that the reader can care about.

Activity 2 — The plot thickens

> Nothing could separate the two. They really were the best of friends. That is until Jo moved in at number 13.

Make notes for three sections in the middle of your story:

- Jo talks with the first friend.
- Jo talks with the second friend.
- The two friends fight because of the lies they have been told.

You need to work out what lies Jo could tell that would lead the friends to fight. The reader needs to be convinced that it is enough to break up two very good friends.

Activity 3 — The resolution

Make notes under these headings.

- How do the friends discover they have been tricked?
- What do they do to make it up?
- What happens to Jo, the liar?

Activity 4 — Get started

Now you have plenty of ideas in your notes for your story. Make a paragraph plan (see page 163) and write your story.

Feedback

I have:
→ learnt a basic structure for story writing
→ made use of some key features of good stories.

177

3 Know how to write instructions

Learning objective

I am learning how to write instructions.

Instructions are a special kind of writing. The purpose of instructions is to tell the reader how to do something. Instructions might tell you, for instance, how to:
- cook something
- make something work
- play a game.

Instructions should be:
- as brief as possible (otherwise people won't read them)
- clear (otherwise people get it wrong).

> **Key term**
>
> **Command verb (imperative)**
> The basic form of a verb used without a subject to give a direction or command. It usually starts the sentence.

Activity 1 Identify the key features of instructions

Look at these instructions for making a cup of tea.

> Put a teabag in a cup.
>
> Pour on boiling water.
>
> Stir and leave for about 3 minutes.
>
> Add milk and sugar as required.

Notice that:
- each sentence begins with a command verb (no subject)
- each step starts on a new line
- the steps have to be in the right order
- it is important not to miss out any steps.

Unit 16 Know how to focus your writing on audience and purpose

1 One step has been missed in these instructions. What was it? Where does it fit in the order?

2 Now write your own instructions for making a cup of instant coffee.

Activity 2 | **Look at 'how to' guides**

We go through life needing to know how to do things. Now we can search the internet and find out how to do almost anything – even how to tell the gender of a pet rat.

Look at this guide on how to survive a dog attack.

1 Try to remain calm.
   Panic may cause the dog to become more aggressive.
2 Shout for help.
   If you are with someone, get them to fetch help.
3 Stand still.
   Running away will make the dog want to chase you.
4 Do not use your arm to distance yourself from the dog.
   The dog may be attracted to snap at it.
5 Do not pull away if the dog bites.
   This will cause more damage to your skin.

Notice how this works. Each direction has a piece of extra information on the next line in italics.

Write your own 'how to' guide. It could be a serious one about something you really know how to do or it could be humorous such as:
- How to avoid being kidnapped by aliens
- How to avoid being kissed by an aunty

Feedback

→ I know the key features of instruction writing

→ I can write a set of clear instructions.

179

4 Know how to write about something you did

Learning objective

I am learning how to write interestingly about my own experiences.

Comedians often say, 'It's not the joke that's funny, it's the way I tell it.' Writing about things you did is the same. It won't be very interesting to your reader unless you write about it well. Good writers can make quite ordinary events into an interesting read.

This kind of writing:
- tells us about a series of events in time order (see pages 163–164)
- uses the first person (I/we)
- seeks to share the writer's experience through specific and vivid description
- includes the writer's thoughts about what happened.

> **Key term**
>
> **Writing in the first person**
> Writing using 'I' or 'we' as the subject, for example: 'I went to the concert'.

Activity 1 Make it vivid

If you want to really share your experience with your reader, you need to paint a picture in words of what it was like.

In this text, choose the words in brackets that you think will make the writing most vivid.

It was my first ever job. I had to start at the factory at 7.30 which was a lot earlier than school. As I left my house, the streets seemed (quiet, empty, deserted). My footsteps on the pavement (sounded loud, echoed hollowly, resounded) as I (hurried, raced, stepped) along. I (was determined, had made up my mind, wanted) not to be late on my first day.

As I entered the factory, I was (amazed, astonished, stunned) by what I saw. White powder lay everywhere. It had collected in (big, huge, deep, mighty) (heaps, clumps, drifts) in every corner. Every surface, every wire had a light, white (covering, topping, coating, crust) like snow.

Unit 16 Know how to focus your writing on audience and purpose

'What is it?' I asked the foreman, pointing and (shouting, bellowing, raising my voice) to be heard over the (din, racket, crashing, roaring, banging) of the machinery.

'Talcum powder, lad. To stop the rubber sticking.'

Activity 2 — Add your thoughts

This is an extract from Rio Ferdinand's autobiography. He is describing his first day at Manchester United.

Putting the Manchester United strip on for the first time, it felt the same as when you got a new kit as a kid. It was exciting. I was tugging at it all over thinking to myself, 'This is how Man United socks are, this is how they feel. This is how their shirts feel. These are their shorts.' Even the texture of it gave me goosebumps.

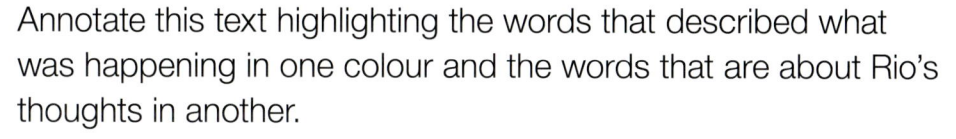

Annotate this text highlighting the words that described what was happening in one colour and the words that are about Rio's thoughts in another.

You should find that you have highlighted more words relating to Rio's thoughts.

Focus your effort

Make sure you include vivid description and remember to write about your thoughts as well as about what happened.

Activity 3 — Your own writing

Rio Ferdinand's first day at Manchester United was a day he will always remember. Write about a day in your life that you remember because it was special in some way. Look at pages 141–142 if you need help to plan your writing.

Feedback

I can:
→ write interestingly about things that have happened to me
→ include my thoughts as well as describing what took place.

181

5 Know how to write information texts

Learning objective

I am learning how to write texts that are designed to give the reader factual information.

Providing factual information is a very important purpose for writing. You will find these kinds of texts in non-fiction books, encyclopaedias, leaflets and on websites.

Information writing often:
- makes use of headings and sub-headings to help the reader find the information required
- starts with the most general facts and then gives more detailed information in the sections/paragraphs that follow
- uses clear and precise language
- is written in the present tense, because it describes how things 'are'.

Activity 1 Look at the structure of information writing

In the article on the opposite page link the features in the right-hand column to the parts of the information text.

Activity 2 Write your own information text

Pick a topic that you can write about in a similar way to the Ants text. For instance, you could look up information about spiders, sharks, horses or mice.

Write your own information text using a plan like this:
- The most general facts about the subject
- Some other important facts
- A fact that could surprise your reader
- An answer to a question that a reader might have
- Facts about one particular example of the topic (for example, one special type of spider)

Key term

Sub-heading
Not the main heading, but a heading at the start of a section or paragraph which sums up what it is about.

Focus your effort
Remember to use sub-headings!

Unit 16 Know how to focus your writing on audience and purpose

Ants

Ants are insects. There are many thousands of species of ants, which live everywhere on the planet except Antarctica.

How ants live

Leafcutter ant transporting a leaf

Most ants live in colonies. They work together doing different jobs. The queen lays eggs. The worker ants look after the eggs and find food. Soldier ants protect the nest. There are a small number of drones whose job is to mate with future queens.

An amazing fact about ants

Ants are incredibly strong. They can lift 20 times their own body weight. If people were this strong they could easily lift up a car.

Are ants just a pest?

Ants can cause a lot of damage if they get into your house and can be very irritating if they invade your picnic. On the other hand, ants are good for the environment in many ways and also provide food for other animals.

Leafcutter ants

This kind of ant feeds only on a special fungus which it farms in its colony. They collect leaves which are cut into tiny pieces and placed in fungus gardens. The largest ants cut leaves, smaller workers chew the leaves and the smallest look after the fungus.

Sub-heading

Very general statement about ants

Section focusing on one example of ant behaviour

Section focusing on a question the reader might have

Examples of the present tense

A fact highlighted to surprise the reader

Short sentence stating a main fact

Example of precise vocabulary

Caption giving information about an illustration

Main heading

Feedback

→ I can write an information text that communicates facts clearly.

6 Know how to write descriptively

Learning objective

I am learning how to write descriptions to engage my reader's imagination and to communicate factual information accurately.

In stories and poems, writers describe things to help the reader picture settings and characters in their own minds. We call these **imaginative descriptions**. These descriptions often include imagery designed to appeal to our senses.

Sometimes we have to write a description that is meant to communicate facts. For example, you might have to describe the damage done to your car in a crash. We call these **factual descriptions**. These descriptions should be clear and accurate.

Activity 1 Identify the features of imaginative description

Label this descriptive passage to show how the writer John Banville has used these key features of descriptive writing:
- adjectives
- adverbs
- specific detail.

> The first thing I saw of them was their motor car, parked on the gravel inside the gate. It was a low-slung, scarred and battered black model with beige leather seats and a big spoked polished wood steering wheel. Books with bleached and dog-eared covers were thrown carelessly on the shelf under the sportily raked back window, and there was a touring map of France, much used.

Unit 16 Know how to focus your writing on audience and purpose

Activity 2 | Be specific

Good writers are very specific when they describe things. Instead of writing:

> There was a fish on the table.

They write:

> On the table lay a huge, wet haddock.

Make these sentences more descriptive by replacing the highlighted words with more specific detail.

- He ate **a bowl of cereal** for breakfast.
- Although it was cold she wore **shorts**.
- A **dog** appeared at the gate.
- The old lady always carried a **bag**.
- She always had her **mobile phone** in her hand.

Activity 3 | Describe characters

In the extract in Activity 1 John Banville starts to describe the Grace family, who are important characters in his book *The Sea*. The car gives us a first idea of what they might be like and then Mr Grace comes out.

> He wore a loose green shirt unbuttoned and khaki shorts and was barefoot. His skin was so deeply tanned by the sun it had a purplish sheen. Even his feet, I noticed were brown on the insteps: the majority of fathers in my experience were fish-belly white below the collar-line. He set his tumbler – ice-blue gin and ice cubes and a lemon slice – at a perilous angle on the roof of the car and opened the passenger door and leaned inside to rummage for something under the dashboard.

Key terms

Specific details
Precise information rather than just general terms.

Imagery
Language used to create an idea in a reader's mind. Imagery can be linked to all five senses.

185

6 Know how to write descriptively

Focus your effort

Make the car match the character of the family member, and remember to use adjectives, adverbs and specific details in your writing.

1 Imagine a new family has moved in near you. Write your own imaginative description.

Start by describing the car parked on the drive and then describe one of the family members who comes out to get something from the car.

Activity 4 Use imagery

Writers can use language to create ideas in our minds that relate to all five of our senses: sight, hearing, touch, taste and smell.

1 Identify the words in this text that connect to each of the five senses.

> As she entered the kitchen, the yeasty smell of baking bread came to her. The bright red display on the oven told her that in three minutes she would be able to take the loaf out and run her fingers over its hot, rough crust.
>
> At last the timer made its sound, like the cry of a distressed bird. Half an hour to cool and then she would cut a thick slice from the loaf, butter it and smear it thickly with sweet, sticky strawberry jam.

2 Write your own description of entering a room in a house using imagery for all five senses.

Activity 5 Look at factual description

With factual description we don't really want the reader to use their imagination to create a picture in their mind; we want them to know exactly what something looks like. For instance:

Draw a square with sides 10 cm long.

This describes the shape exactly so you could draw it.

Unit 16 Know how to focus your writing on audience and purpose

1 Look at this factual description.

> **Black backpack for laptop or tablet**
>
> Made from heavy-duty black nylon, waterproof fabric
>
> Weighs less than a kilo when empty
>
> Padded straps for comfort while carrying
>
> Dedicated compartments that fit both a 15.6" laptop and an iPad or tablet
>
> Spacious middle compartment stores folders, books, headphones or extra clothing
>
> Zipper pockets provide cord, smartphone and small accessory storage so they do not disappear into the bottom of the bag
>
> Front compartment features storage pockets and a zipper pocket

Identify these key features of factual description in the text:
- Exact details including measurements
- Precise vocabulary
- Facts not opinions
- Conciseness (tells you what you need to know and no more)

Activity 6 Write a witness statement

One time when you might have to make a factual description is if you witnessed a crime. The police might ask you to describe a person you saw.

This is a picture of a man you saw commit a robbery in the street. Make a checklist of the features that would be helpful to the police and then write your description.

> **Feedback**
>
> I can:
> → write an imaginative description
> → include imagery in a description
> → write a clear and accurate factual description.

7 Know how to write explanations

Learning objective

I am learning how to write a clear explanation of a process.

We live in a complicated world. Scientists and others have made huge progress in finding out how everything works. Explaining the complex processes that go on around us all the time in a way that is easily understood is a key writing skill.

Features of writing to explain are:
- breaking down a process into a series of steps
- using time and cause and effect connectives
- using special vocabulary, which might need to be explained when first used
- using diagrams with captions/labels.

Activity 1   Identify the features of explanations

Match the features listed opposite to parts of the text below.

What does your heart do?

The heart is a muscle inside your chest. It works like a kind of pump and its job is to send blood around the body.

First the heart fills with blood.

Then the heart muscle contracts – this is a heartbeat – squeezing the blood out.

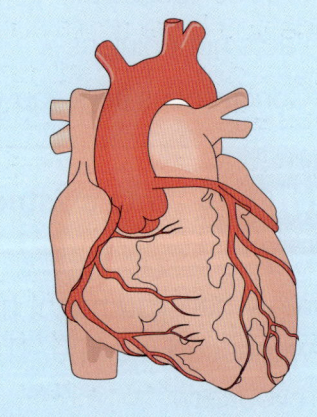

The heart is about the size of your fist

Next the blood takes oxygen and nutrients (that is food) to all parts of the body so that, for instance, muscles can work.

Blood also has the job of helping to remove waste products from the body.

Finally the blood returns to the heart so that it can be pumped around the body again.

The heart has to keep working like this 24 hours a day.

Unit 16 Know how to focus your writing on audience and purpose

Final concluding statement
An illustration with a caption that adds information
A series of steps to explain a process
Cause and effect connectives
General statement to introduce the explanation
Special vocabulary that needs explaining
Time connectives

Activity 2 — Write a scientific explanation

This diagram shows how water circulates on our planet – it is called the water cycle.

Write an explanation of the water cycle to go with this diagram. Use the explanation structure and the features that you explored in Activity 1.

Activity 3 — Explain an everyday process

Imagine you have a pet alien living with you who does not understand anything about the everyday processes of human life. It keeps asking you questions like, 'Why do you sometimes use a vacuum cleaner in your bedroom?'

Your explanation might be:

> A vacuum cleaner is a machine that is designed to remove dirt from carpets. This is how I come to use it in my room.
>
> Over time bits of dirt collect on my bedroom carpet.
>
> Then my mother comes in and says, 'This room needs a vacuum.'
>
> Because she didn't sound cross I don't do anything about it.
>
> About a week later she comes in and says, 'This carpet is filthy, get it cleaned or no pocket money.'
>
> So, finally, I get the vacuum cleaner out to suck up the dirt.

Write your explanation to the alien of another everyday process. Choose your own or you could try:

- Why do you take the dog for a walk?
- Why do your always torment your brother/sister?

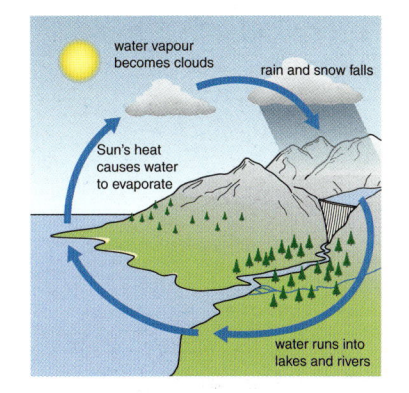

Feedback

I can write a clear explanation of a process.

189

8 Know how to write to discuss and persuade

Learning objective

I am learning how to write essays to:
- *outline, investigate and explore a topic*
- *try to persuade the reader of a point of view.*

An essay is a piece of writing in which you give your views and ideas on a given topic. There are many different kinds of essay. You could be asked to write a history essay explaining why the Roman army was so successful. You could be asked to write an English essay about school uniform. You might have strong views about school uniform so you might write the essay to persuade your reader to agree with you.

Activity 1 Plan an essay

Essays are usually planned with this structure:

Essay structure	
Part 1	A paragraph that introduces the topic • Includes a sentence that summarises what you want to say about the topic
Part 2	A number of paragraphs that deal with aspects of the topic – these include evidence, facts and opinions • Paragraphs often come in order of importance. • Paragraphs are linked through connectives.
Part 3	A paragraph that sums up the topic without bringing in any more information.

Unit 16 Know how to focus your writing on audience and purpose

Read this student's essay about homework and use the labels to find and identify the key features.

Homework

Homework is the work that students are asked to do outside of school hours. It does not actually have to be done at home. Hardly anyone likes homework but it is a necessary evil.

Students do not usually like homework because they feel they have been working at school all day and enough is enough! Also, time spent doing homework limits their leisure activities. However, students who want to do well in their exams do accept the need for homework.

Surprisingly, many teachers also dislike homework. It means extra work setting it, chasing it and marking it. It is a constant source of conflict both with students who fail to do it and with school managers who demand that the homework timetable is followed. On the other hand teachers know that without homework all the work will not be covered and the students may fail.

Another group affected by homework is parents. When it makes their children unhappy, when they have to try and help with it and when they get letters from school complaining about it, they don't like it. Nevertheless parents often ask schools to set more homework and many parents feel reassured by the idea that their children will be kept busy every evening with school work instead of doing goodness knows what on their computers or going out.

It seems that nobody closely connected with homework is entirely happy about it. On the other hand, useful homework is necessary to succeed at school.

Key features:

- paragraph that introduces the topic
- a sentence that summarises what you want to say about the topic
- paragraphs that deal with aspects of the topic
- evidence, facts and opinions
- links between paragraphs
- connectives that allow more than one point of view
- concluding paragraph that sums up the topic

8 Know how to write to discuss and persuade

> **Activity 2** — Plan and write your own essay

Key term

Expository essay
A piece of writing that seeks to outline, investigate and explore a topic.

Your topic is:

> Is it right for parents to limit children's use of phones and computers?

Your essay should consider this issue from the point of view of both parents and children.

You can use this grid to make your plan. It follows the essay structure on page 188.

Is it right for parents to limit children's use of phones and computers?	
Part 1	•
Part 2	• • •
Part 3	•

> **Activity 3** — Identify the features of persuasive essays

Key term

Persuasive essay
Writing that puts one argument forward and seeks to make the reader agree.

Some essays are not written to explore all sides of a topic but to convince the reader to believe a particular thing or agree with a particular point of view.

The structure of this kind of essay is normally the same as the expository essay but persuasive essays have certain typical features:

- The writer states their point of view with great confidence.
- Other evidence or opinions are not mentioned or are only mentioned so they can be dismissed.
- The language can be more emotive and writing techniques such as repetition or the rule of three may be used.

Unit 16 Know how to focus your writing on audience and purpose

1 Read this persuasive essay and use the labels to identify the typical features of persuasive writing. To help you, look at unit 14.6.

> Boxing is not really a sport, it is just a spectacle put on for sick-minded people who like to see someone hurt.
>
> All sports, whether they are individual sports like tennis or team games like football, are about defeating the opponent, but boxing is an activity in which the main point is to hurt your opponent. You actually win by doing this! You may argue that physical contact and injury is part of many sports, but only boxers must injure their opponent to win.
>
> Some boxers have died in the ring. Many more have suffered brain damage from repeated blows to the head. Bang, bang, bang! Each punch violently shakes the brain inside the skull and, slowly but surely, the damage is done until the boxer becomes 'punch drunk'. As many as 20 per cent of ex-boxers suffer the symptoms of this: memory loss, speech problems and difficulties with walking.
>
> Do we really want to be entertained by the sight of two men (or women, believe it or not!) trying to batter each other into a bloody pulp? I think not.
>
> Let us ban this so-called sport now.

Key features:
- emotive language
- key facts
- repetition
- strongly-expressed personal view
- rhetorical question
- punchy, short sentence to conclude

Activity 4 Write a persuasive essay

Think of a topic that you feel strongly about. It could be something like bullying or the mistreatment of animals or the protection of the environment. Write a persuasive essay about it.

Focus your effort

Remember to use the essay structure discussed on page 188. Include some of the features of persuasive writing.

Feedback

I can:
→ plan using the essay structure
→ write an essay that investigates and explores a topic
→ write an essay that tries to persuade the reader to agree with my view.

193

9 Know when to use formal and informal writing

Learning objective

I am learning to adapt my writing style to match my reader's expectations.

People wear different clothes for different occasions. You wear one thing for a wedding and another for cleaning a bike. Likewise with writing: we choose different styles of writing for different readers. It is important to choose the right level of formality if you want to gain the respect of your reader. There is a kind of scale from very formal to very informal. All writing fits somewhere on this scale.

Key terms

Formal writing
Used in schools, in the world of work and in books.

Informal writing
More like speech and may include non-Standard English.

Legal and official documents	Business letters Job applications	Everyday writing School work	Friendly messages	Messages to people you know very well
---→ Formal writing ---→		---→ ---→ Informal writing ---→ ---→		
Standard English	Standard English	Standard English	Some non-Standard English	Some non-Standard English, slang and abbreviations such as text speak

Activity 1 — Recognise formal and informal writing

Rate these sentences from 1 to 5 where 1 is very formal and 5 is very informal.

a) U R L8

b) I regret to inform you that because of late payment we shall proceed to legal action.

c) The Second World War began in 1939 and continued until 1945.

d) I consider myself well qualified to work for your company.

e) Hi, Mrs Jones. The postman left your parcel at our house. Cheers Jen

Unit 16 Know how to focus your writing on audience and purpose

f) Parking prohibited.

g) Please don't throw litter into my garden.

h) Wow – that was some photo you sent me

i) It is a requirement that all visitors shall report to reception.

j) Went to town. Shops were BUZZING. Knackered now.

Activity 2 — Identify formal and informal words

Using certain words/phrases can make your writing more or less formal.

Identify which word in each pair is more formal.

get	receive
don't	do not
commence	begin
get in touch	contact
broken	busted
bike	bicycle
make sure	ensure
inform me	fill me in
check	verify
kids	children

Activity 3 — Match the style to the reader

How formal would you be in these writing tasks?

Decide whether each is very formal, formal, informal, or very informal.

- History essay for school
- Letter to the headteacher apologising for bad behaviour in assembly

9 Know when to use formal and informal writing

- Internet message to your best friend
- Email message to someone your own age you don't know very well
- Email message to an adult you don't know very well
- Some notes you made for yourself
- Noticeboard message for other students in your class
- Email to your MP asking for help with a community problem
- Witness statement for the police
- A note left for your mum explaining where you are

Activity 4 | Use formal writing

This email to Mr Jones – Janice's employer – should be written in a more formal style.

Re-write it to match better with the intended reader (who is in fact a bit old-fashioned).

> Hi Boss
>
> Just wanna put you in the picture about tomorrow. Can't turn up at the shop cos of problems with the littl'un. He's throwing up everywhere – right poorly.
>
> Sorry to let you down but that's kids eh. Sure I'll be in next week tho cheers Jan

Activity 5 | Use Standard English

If you are writing formally, it is important to use Standard English. Standard English is a national form of the language and differs in grammar and vocabulary from local speech which varies widely across the UK.

Re-write these sentences in Standard English.

Unit 16 Know how to focus your writing on audience and purpose

1 It was them fizzy drinks what made her fat.
2 You ain't seen nothing yet.
3 He done his homework.
4 The team played good but the other side were more better.
5 Me and my friend always walk home together.
6 They wanted the money for theirselves.
7 The children played nice together.
8 He were the best swimmer in the group.
9 Once the tree has fell over it can be used for firewood.
10 Nobody couldn't fix that car.

Activity 6 Write formally and informally

Imagine you have been away to some athletics trials or to a singing audition. You have been picked for England or you get through to the final which will be on TV.

Write three email messages to let people know about your success and what will happen next.

- Email 1 (formal) to your headteacher (she allowed you time off school to go to the trials/audition)
- Email 2 (informal) to an uncle or aunt who has been giving you a lot of help with training
- Email 3 (very informal) to your best friend

Focus your effort

Remember to use more formal vocabulary and Standard English when you are writing formally.

Feedback

I can:
- write an imaginative description using key features
- include imagery in a description
- write a clear and accurate factual description.

The publisher would like to thank the following for permission to reproduce copyright material:

Although every effort has been made to ensure that website addresses are correct at time of going to press, Hodder Education cannot be held responsible for the content of any website mentioned. It is sometimes possible to find a relocated web page by typing in the address of the home page for a website in the URL window of your browser.

Orders: please contact Bookpoint Ltd, 130 Milton Park, Abingdon, Oxon OX14 4SB. Telephone: (44) 01235 827720. Fax: (44) 01235 400454. Lines are open 9.00–17.00, Monday to Saturday, with a 24-hour message answering service. Visit our website at www.hoddereducation.co.uk

© Sarah Forrest, David White 2014
First published in 2014 by
Hodder Education
An Hachette UK Company,
338 Euston Road
London NW1 3BH

Impression number	5	4	3	2	1
Year	2018	2017	2016	2015	2014

All rights reserved. Apart from any use permitted under UK copyright law, no part of this publication may be reproduced or transmitted in any form or by any means, electronic or mechanical, including photocopying and recording, or held within any information storage and retrieval system, without permission in writing from the publisher or under licence from the Copyright Licensing Agency Limited. Further details of such licences (for reprographic reproduction) may be obtained from the Copyright Licensing Agency Limited, Saffron House, 6–10 Kirby Street, London EC1N 8TS.

Illustrations by Cathy Fisher/Barking Dog Art
Typeset in ITC Garamond Std Light 9/12 by Integra Software Services Pvt. Ltd., Pondicherry, India

Printed in Italy

A catalogue record for this title is available from the British Library

ISBN 978 1 444 16901 0

Acknowledgments:

p.4: Martin Robinson, 'Careful who you throw snowballs at! Firemen take revenge on teenagers by giving them a drenching with Power hosery', from *Mail Online* (21 January, 2013); **p.5**: from Manchester United Museum and Tour leaflet; 'Isaac's story' from *Shout magazine* (21-22 May, 2013); **p.6**: Banner with title 'Funding the Future', and picture of Mo Farah from *http://www.firstnews.co.uk/news/sport-sponsorships-time-for-a-rethink-i9240*; **p.9**: Stockport Metropolitan Borough Council, 'Children's Explorers Tours' from http:www.stockport.gov.uk/2013/3000/558305/524334/stockportmuseumsgalleriesexhibitionseventsguidespringandsummer2013 from *Stockport Museums & Events Guide, Spring/Summer 2013*; **p.9**: Virginia Blackburn, from *The Unauthorised Robert Pattinson Inside Out* (Michael O'Mara Books, 2009); **p.11**: Palace Theatre & Opera House, Manchester, 'Lion King', realia from *http://www.wantamedia.com/downloads/atg_ptm9_060313/index.html#/2*; **p.13**: 'This is the dramatic moment a heroic passer-by rescued a two-year boy…' from *http://www.thesun.co.uk/sol/homepage/news/4922 648/child-two-rescued-after-toddling-onto-roof-40ft-above-ground.html*, reproduced by permission of News UK; **p.16**: Adam Arnell, One page layout including photographs from Tectonic processes from *KS3 Success - Geography Study Guide* (Letts, 2004); **p.18**: Moniza Alvi,from 'Presents from my aunts in Pakistan' from *The Country At My Shoulder (Oxford Poets)*, (Oxford University Press, 1993); **p.23**: Lego Friends Instruction Booklet from *http://cache.lego.com/bigdownloads/buildinginstructions/6001988.pdf*; Jeff Kinney, One page layout from September, including pictures from *Diary of a Wimpy Kid* (Puffin Books, 2008), reproduced by permission of Penguin Books Ltd; **p.26**: Matt Anniss, 'Go For It! Tell Everyone' from *Find Your Talent. Make a Podcast!* (Franklin Watts, 2012); **p.27**: Catherine Forde, from *Fat Boy Swim* (Egmont Books, 2003); **p.28**: 'Magic Kingdom Park' from *Thomas Cook Florida and Las Vegas 2013-2014* brochure from *http://www.brochure-store.co.uk/Brochures/Thomas-Cook/TCTTFLS114/walt-disney-world-resort/Pages22*; **p.31**: Playfactore poster from *www.playfactore.com*; **p.32**: Chester Zoo, 'Peek-a-BOO! poster; **p.33**: Young Driver Training Ltd, 'You don't have to wait until you're 17 to get behind the wheel of a car', poster from www.youngdriver.eu; **p.36-39**: Benjamin Mee, from *We Bought a Zoo* (HarperCollins, 2012); **pp.43**: Christopher Paolini, from *Eragon* (Doubleday, 2004); **pp.44-47**: Eoin Colfer, from *Artemis Fowl* (Viking, 2001); **pp.48-49**: J.K. Rowling, from *Harry Potter and the Philosopher's Stone* (Bloomsbury Publishing, 1997); **p.50**: David Almond, from *Skellig* (Hodder Children's Books, 1998); **p.55**: Sonya Hartnett, from *The Midnight Zoo* (Walker Books, 2010); **pp.54, 60**: Ffyona Campbell, from *On Foot Through Africa* (Orion, 1994); **p.56, 57**: Jeremy Clarkson, from *Don't Stop Me Now* (Penguin Books, 2008); **p.58**: Roald Dahl, from *Charlie and the Chocolate Factory* (Puffin Books, 1973); **p.59**: John Steinbeck, from *Of Mice and Men* (Penguin Classics, 2006); **p.66**: 'Help us beat heart disease your way. Volunteer today' leaflet, reproduced with the permssion of the British Heart Foundation; **p.68**: 'Benfica Need Goals' from *MATCH Magazine* (April 30-May 6); **p.70**: Olivia Ababio, Review of 'Top 5 Christmas Movies' from *http://www.live-magazine.co.uk/2012/12/top-5-christmas-movies*; **p.72**: Susan Green, from *The Truth about Verity Sparks*; **p.73**: Geraldine McCaughrean, from *The Orchard Book of Greek Myths* (Orchard Books, 2013); **p.74**: Lemony Snicket, from *A Series of Unfortunate Events: The Bad Beginning* (HarperCollins Children's Books, 1999); **p.77**: Sally Murphy, 'My head whirls', extract from *Toppling* (Candlewick Press, 2012), reproduced by permission of Walker Books; H. G. Wells, from *The War of the Worlds* (Heinemann, 1898); **p.78**: Louis Sachar from *Holes* (Bloomsbury Publishing, 2000); **p.79**: Charlie Brooker, from 'Who are these people and what are they wearing?' (April 30, 2007) from *Dawn of the Dumb* (Faber & Faber, 2007), © Charlie Brooker, 2007; **p.81**: William Golding, from *Lord of the Flies* (Faber & Faber, 1954); **p.82**: Alfred Noyes, from 'The Highwayman' from *The Highwayman* (Oxford University Press, 1981); **pp.84, 85**: George Orwell, from *Animal Farm* (Martin Secker & Warburg, 1945); **p.86**: Barack Obama, 'Yes we can…' speech (2009) **p.88**: Willy Russell, 'Sammy' extract from *Blood Brothers* (Methuen Drama, n/e, 2001), reproduced by permission of Bloomsbury Publishing Plc; **pp.90, 91, 92**: Michael Morpurgo, from *Private Peaceful* (HarperCollins, 2003); **p.156**: James Reeves, 'Slowly' from *Hurdy-Gurdy* (Heinemann, 1961); **p.156**: Ted Hughes, from 'Wind' from *New Selected Poems 1957-1994* (Faber & Faber, 1995); **p.158**: Andrew Young, 'A Windy Day', extract from *Selected Poems* (Carcanet Press, 1998), copyright © The Estate of Andrew Young; **p.179**: 'Try to remain calm', extract adapted from *http://www.mirror.co.uk/news/uk-news//how-to-survive-a-dog-attack-770133*, reproduced by permission of Mirrorpix; **pp.180-181**: Rio Ferdinand, from *Rio: My Story* (Headline, 2006); **p.185**: John Banville, from *The Sea* (Picador, 2005).

Every effort has been made to trace or contact all copyright holders. The publishers will be pleased to rectify any errors or omissions at the earliest opportunity.

Photo credits:

p.12: © Newsteam / SWNS Group; **p.14**: © GTV Archive/REX; **p19**: © Yamini Chao/Photodisc/Getty Images; **p.35**: © Warren Goldswain/Getty Images/iStockphoto/Thinkstock; **p.37**: © kerstiny/Fotolia; **p.39**: tiger© xy/Fotolia; **p.40**: © Tetyana / Fotolia; **p.42**: © Rex Features; **p.53**: © nickolae/Fotolia; **p.54**: David Crump/Associated Newsp/REX; **p.58**: ullstein bild/TopFoto; **p.63**: © Schotter Studio/Fotolia; **p.64**: © klagyivik/Fotolia; **p.69**: © JiSIGN/Fotolia; **p.70**: Everett Collection/REX; **p.71t**: © 20th Century Fox Film Corp./courtesy Everett Collection/Rex Features; **p.71b**: © Universal/DNA/Working Title / The Kobal Collection; **p.73**: © Bettmann/CORBIS; **p.76**: © leelana/Fotolia; **p.78**: © piyathep/Fotolia; **p.79**: SPG/Rex Features; **p.83**: © Mary Evans Picture Library / Alamy; **p.85**: © AF archive / Alamy; **p.86**: Alex Wong/Getty Images; **p.89**: © 14ktgold/Fotolia; **p.90**: © Topham Picturepoint/TopFoto; **p.92**: © Roger-Viollet / TopFoto; **p.98**: © Getty Images/iStockphoto/Thinkstock; **p.101**: © Erni/Fotolia; **p.102**: © Jacek Chabraszewski/Fotolia; **p.103**: © beemanja/Fotolia; **p.104**: © prudkov/Fotolia; **p.107t**: © Microstock Man/Fotolia; **p.107b**: © victorhabbick/Fotolia; **p.108**: © The Granger Collection / TopFoto; **p.111**: © tinadefortunata/Fotolia; **p.112**: © bloomua/Fotolia; **p.114**: © solovyova/Fotolia; **p.116**: fork: © AlexAvich – Fotolia, spade: © mbongo – Fotolia, rake: © Ingram Publishing Limited, hoe: © Beth Van Trees – Fotolia, trowel: © keerati – Fotolia; **p.117**: © Rebecca Hanson/Fotolia; **p.119**: © gl0ck/Fotolia; **p.121**: © leonmaraisphoto/Fotolia; **p.123**: © Okea – Fotolia; **p.124**: © Dmitriy Shpilko/iStockphoto/Thinkstock; **p.127**: © Adam Gregor/Fotolia; **p.130**: © Igor Mojzes/Fotolia; **p.150**: © Maridav/Fotolia; **p.151**: © sumnersgraphicsinc – Fotolia; **p.152**: © Ingram Publishing Company; **p.155**: © Bikeworldtravel/Fotolia; **p.157**: © Brendan Howard – Fotolia; **p.159**: © KoMa – Fotolia; **p.161**: grafix132/Fotolia; **p.163**: © Eric Gevaert - Fotolia; **p.164**: © Getty Images/Purestock/Thinkstock; **p.166**: © determined/Fotolia; **p.167**: © Getty Images/The Bridgeman Art Library; **p.170**: © vvoe – Fotolia; **p.178**: © Imagestate Media (John Foxx); **p.179**: © petert2 – Fotolia; **p.181**: © Ben Radford/Getty Images; **p.183**: © Eric Isselée – Fotolia; **p.185**: © Jacek Nowak / Alamy; **p.186**: ©Studio Gi – Fotolia; **p.191**: ©Ant Clausen – Fotolia; **p.193**: © nickp37/iStockphoto/Thinkstock.